Martin Lyster

was born in St Albans in 1 ...... at Oxford University, he became involved in the Dangerous Sports Club shortly after its foundation, and became a leading organiser. Taking responsibility for the Club's bungee jumping displays, he developed the techniques of safe jumping which are now the foundation of a worldwide industry. He also helped organise the surrealist ski races in St Moritz and piloted several of the Club's eye-catching inflatables, including a flying kangaroo, and a giant amphibious sphere containing a tea table.

He is an expert skydiver, BASE jumper and an experienced pilot of gliders, hang-gliders, and balloons. He has parachuted from Clifton suspension bridge, the Cheddar Gorge, and some of the highest cliffs, bridges and towers in Britain and America. In 1989, he was among thirty individuals shortlisted to become the first British astronaut. He is newly married and lives on a narrowboat moored on the Oxford canal.

The Strange
Adventures
of the
Dangerous
Sports Club

This edition published in Great Britain in 1997 by
The Do-Not Press
PO Box 4215
London SE23 2QD

A paperback original

ISBN 1 899344 28 4

British Library Cataloguing in Publication Data. A catalogue record for
this book is available from the British Library.

Printed and bound in Great Britain by The Guernsey Press Co. Ltd

The Strange
Adventures
of the
Dangerous
Sports Club

Martin Lyster

THE DO-NOT
PRESS

Introduction

'I know that history will be good to me, because
I am going to write it.'
– Winston Churchill, 1945

One of the freedoms we enjoy is the freedom to take personal risks, deciding for ourselves where to draw the line; while society as a whole tends to pull the other way, constantly seeking to make us all safer. So, in writing a song of praise to the joys of dangerous sports, I realise that I may give offence to those who see bicycle helmets, decaffeination and traffic calming as symbols of progress.

Sometimes it seems that the line of social acceptability between healthy adventure and reckless folly is closing in a little more every year, but the news is not all bad. A boom is under way in many new sports which involve risk, and there is mainstream coverage today of sports which, just a short time ago, were only reported as lunatic-fringe activities, with viewers ordered not to try them at home. As the dispute goes on over whether racing cars which kill their drivers should be painted in the colours of cigarette brands which kill their smokers, we continue to struggle in a difficult relationship with personal and collective danger. This book, the story of some bizarre and flamboyant attempts to consummate the marriage of risk and fun, is my own contribution to our understanding of the human need to walk on the wild side now and then.

I would like to thank all those who have contributed, especially those who shared with me their memories of Club events, or who helped with my research in other ways, and who gave me so many quotes and photographs. To some extent this story is a group

8

effort, as was the Club itself. I am particularly indebted to Mark Chamberlain, Chris Baker, Dan Gold, Alan Weston, Xan Rufus-Isaacs, Jerome Fack, Jean Boenish, Mike Fitzroy and my wife Ruth. Any inaccuracies which remain are my own. The people and events I have chosen to describe, and the light in which I show them, reflect my personal view. The Club ran on a heady cocktail of Champagne and adrenaline, and it is not surprising if individuals remember events differently. Not everyone involved will agree with my opinions, but given the vast body of film, TV, radio, book, newspaper and magazine coverage of the Club, there is room for all to have their say.

Finally, I would like to dedicate this book to the memory of Graham Chapman, Willy Purcell, Tommy Leigh-Pemberton and Carl Boenish.

The Strange Adventures of
The Dangerous Sports Club

1.

A Short Visit to the Real World

'One day, it will have to be officially admitted that what we have called Reality is an even greater illusion than the world of dreams.'
– Salvador Dali

Probably the first telephone number you learn as a child is 999, although you hope never to have to dial it. Similarly, if you go skydiving, you are trained in the use of the reserve parachute before you make your first jump. You never expect your main parachute to let you down, but if it does, you know what to do.

One Saturday afternoon at my local skydiving club, on my 173rd jump, my main parachute came out with a tangle half way up the lines, preventing the canopy opening. I immediately decided to abandon it. I grabbed the release, pulled it, and went back into free-fall, ready to try my luck with the reserve. I arched my back and spread my arms out wide, so as not to tumble. I was falling head first, looking straight down, and the ground below began to rush at me, blurring with speed as if it were a carpet being pulled away in all directions at once. One part of the airfield remained still, just getting larger, and I knew this point was directly below me. I pulled the reserve ripcord.

I had jumped with my three regular team-mates to attempt a sequence of free-fall formations, and we had split up just a few seconds earlier, separating so that we could open our parachutes. One of them was still in view, and I saw her reaching up for the control lines of her parachute, which had opened as normal. She was still the laid-back, high-spirited team-mate who had given me a friendly free-fall kiss just before the group broke up, and was probably already looking ahead to that night's partying. Her carpet wasn't being pulled.

My own high spirits had been rudely interrupted. I was suddenly somewhere else, in a world of entirely different priorities. Five seconds before, a thousand feet higher, our Saturday night partying had been in my mind too. Now it was replaced with more immediate concerns. I was no longer worried about finding a job, my thinning hair, or my final exams. All that mattered was what I did *now*. The parachute failure had snatched me out of my good, Saturday afternoon mood like a slap in the face. Gravity has no patience. No begging or bargaining can extend its deadlines by a millisecond. You have to make your decision, and then carry it out. You must act straight away, and you'd better get it right, or else. This is a pass/fail test, and you have seven seconds to answer the question. Six. Five...

The reserve parachute opened firmly and I sank deep into my harness. The moment passed; I now had a routine landing ahead of me, and an evening's fun to look forward to. In fact, I would buy an extra round of beers for my friends, the tradition on such occasions. I felt a slight twinge and realised I had pulled a muscle by arching my back. One of the team followed my abandoned parachute to the ground, so I wouldn't lose it. That's what friends are for.

I had passed the unexpected test, and as a reward I was back in my ordinary world of Saturday night parties, making ends meet, doing my laundry, and all the rest of my little routines. I was glad about that, but I did not regret my brief visit to that other world; a world where the body does whatever it has to and complains later; where the brain is focused on the moment because something important depends on it; and where the blood runs fast and hot.

Some people talk about the 'Real World', usually when accusing each other of not living in it; but I knew that I had briefly visited a world of absolute, concrete reality. A world where certainty is as solid as the ground below, and where the only rules are the unbreakable laws of gravity, motion and the elements. I like it there. In that world I am decisive and effective; I don't pass the buck, dither, or put things off. I just do my best, without feeling afraid, weak, or inadequate. Those feelings belong somewhere else, back in the safe, organised, comfortable, everyday world.

It is a place I, like many others, have made a habit of visiting, although the ticket price can be high, and for the careless or unlucky, the return half is not always valid. I have sought out the company of others who go there too, and joined a Club whose members regard excursions there as an art form. It is, though, a world some people do their best to avoid. Although they may be dragged there unwillingly by one of life's nasty surprises, they don't like it, and they regard purposeful exploration of this region as a sign of madness.

Nobody wants a parachute malfunction, of course, any more than a mountaineer wants to fall down a crevasse, or a sailor to be caught in a gale. It is just a possibility you accept as part of the territory. In fact, a successful reserve opening is not a narrow escape from death, it is simply an occasion when you have gone further than usual into the real world; maybe further than you wanted to go. Such an experience takes you far over the horizon, to a region which you may not have seen before, and that is why some say that a person who has been there knows more than one who has not. This may sound like daredevils' bravado (and to some extent it is), but beneath the posturing lies a truth. The knowledge gained in this way, though, is self-knowledge, of no value except to the self. It cannot be written down.

*

Since the Montgolfiers first rose into the air, Amundsen arrived at the South Pole, Hilary and Tensing stood on the summit of Everest, and American astronauts used the moon as a golf course, the casual observer might feel that there are few new places left to explore. Not so; the exciting domain of this very real world that exists just outside the everyday, offers infinite opportunities for those who choose to look there. This kind of exploration may lead up dead ends more often than not, and few of the trails are paved with gold. However, the journey is worthwhile for itself, which is reason enough for explorers to set out, and for others to wish them well.

The Dangerous Sports Club set out to find new paths into this real world, and to do so in a way which would allow us, we hoped, to bring back from it something of value to others as well as ourselves. In this respect, we considered our exploration to be artistic. Over the years, we found one or two new main roads, a few scenic routes and any number of blind alleys; but the exploration was, above all, fun, and what we brought back often caught the imagination of a wide audience. This may have been because the veneer of eccentricity made us entertaining to watch – but there is more to this than just being silly. True eccentricity involves a degree of lateral thinking that is the essence of creativity. We cherished the hope that our adventures stirred the creative juices in others, because those juices are what make us more than a bunch of self-replicating robots.

During its exploration of the real world, the Club grew and spread to include a rich variety of people, taking on a life of its own. In an age when the shrill cry of *There Is No Alternative!* seemed to drown other voices, we spent our energies finding alternatives. In a culture which sees danger as an evil, even the name 'Dangerous Sports Club' verged on the subversive. Our society has gained much by making itself as safe as possible, but at the expense of denying part of our animal nature. We choose to limit ourselves in our daily lives, restricting our behaviour with laws and regulations which, like a fence before the cliff edge, keep us from the point of real danger. Any venture outside this comfortable zone is often considered foolish escapism, maybe something to be punished.

Disobeying the breakable rules of man invites restraint, to protect us lest we are tempted to defy the hard, unbending laws of nature. And yet we evolved out there in the real world, and are born with all the responses we need to deal with it. Like it or not, most people need to exercise those responses sometimes, even if it involves breaking a rule or two. The Dangerous Sports Club was devoted to swimming against the tide in this way – but to some people, that's the only way worth swimming.

2.

The Dangerous Sports Club

'Sport is not about being wrapped up in cotton
wool. Sport is about adapting to the unexpected
and being able to modify plans at the last minute.
Sport, like all life, is about taking your chances.'
– Roger Bannister

It was a bright, clear afternoon. The cold Alpine air condensed
into a knot of onlookers. Chris Baker tolerated the small crowd
with the air of amused detachment that comes naturally to an
instinctive spectator at the theatre of human behaviour. His hang-
glider always aroused casual curiosity, wherever he chose to
transform it from a spindly collection of poles, wires and nylon,
into a thing of grace, capable of flight. Things of grace were rare
enough in the late-Seventies, and the hang-glider had the irresistible combination of novelty and elegance.

Chris had rejected the easy path in life offered him by a public
school education and an old family business. The hang-glider was
the latest in a succession of machines he had experimented with in
the hope that they would provide him with the stimulation he
needed, and was the most promising so far. He took it with him on
a trip to the Alpine resort of Klosters, hoping that flying in the
mountains would make an enjoyable diversion from skiing. In
1977, hang-gliders were difficult to fly; they were unpredictable,
easy to stall, and sometimes fell apart in mid-air. Against this,
Chris had the twin blessings of good luck and instinctively correct
reactions, so useful to those fliers who use their own legs as an
undercarriage.

Two of the onlookers introduced themselves as David Kirke
and Ed Hulton. David had an easy, genial manner, betrayed only

by his slightly bulging eyes, and he had the gift of being able to charm almost anybody with apparently effortless ease. Ed was large, dark, and communicated more by presence than words. He had the melancholy air of a man who could afford to rent happiness occasionally, but who was not sure he would ever work out how to create it for himself.

David and Ed were old friends from their student days at Oxford University. They had met there in the late-Sixties while studying English. Both had public school backgrounds. Like Chris, however, neither David nor Ed had been moulded into the usual shape by these institutions. While they moved easily in the lofty social circles from which privileged Britons traditionally looked down on others, they both identified more with Mad Dogs than with English Gentlemen. For one thing, there was their hobby.

Behind the front rank of aviation pioneers, such as Yuri Gagarin, Chuck Yeager, and the Wright Brothers, stand a band of heroes whose achievements are none the less important for being less famous. George Cayley and Otto Lilienthal, for example, were nineteenth-century glider-builders. They worked in wood, wire and doped fabric. Their foot-launched flying machines, which paved the way for the development of powered aircraft, flew like today's hang-gliders. Both men had the foibles of gentleman-engineers; Cayley disdained actual flight, ordering a footman to be his test pilot, while Lilienthal was so keen on flying that he had a hill constructed specially to launch his machines.

Fascinated by these experiments, David and Ed instinctively realised that they wanted to join the ranks of such pioneers. They started out by building recreations of two wooden gliders from turn-of-the-century plans they found in a library. They crashed them both. Then they approached Chris, that afternoon on a Swiss mountainside, asking for an opportunity to crash his hang-glider. Since he was always a curious observer of people and their self-delusions, Chris decided this would be a sufficiently amusing entertainment that he was willing to risk the 'kite'. Offering David a flight the next morning, Chris finished his screwing-together and clipping-on, picked up the hang-glider and took off. As Chris sailed magnificently into the air, Ed and David watched with newly-opened eyes; here was a flying machine which was almost the perfect instrument of personal freedom. It was a superb conveyance from the crowded valley of safety and everyday life, to the lonely heights of the Real World. It was elegant; it was dangerous. It had style.

The next day, in the cold light of morning, Chris decided to take David just half way up the mountain and launch him from there. He gave David a few words of advice on the use of the control bar, and sent him sliding downhill. As many first-time pilots find, hang-gliders do not always want to move in a straight line during take off. Chris smiled at the usual small herd of spectators, who quickly backed off when David swerved downhill and into the air, making a short flight and, for his first time, a safe landing.

Flying brings on a thirst. Cementing their friendship over a drink, the three men discussed their mutual interest in stimulation, and disappointment with the normal ways of getting it. David and Ed had just come from St Moritz, where they had tried the much-vaunted Cresta Run. The Cresta is an ice track, which you ride lying down on a small sled which looks like a tin tray with runners. They had enjoyed it, but felt the reputation of the Cresta was bigger than the experience. David sneered that it was just a way for German industrialists to impress their mistresses. Hang-gliding was new and full of promise, but was already starting to be licensed, regulated and restricted. There was still time to do something new in this field, but they could see the day fast approaching when hang-glider pilots would be limited to improving, by a few seconds or kilometres, on what others had done before.

All three of them had long known that many of the more interesting sports were technically possible long before they were actually attempted – all that was missing was the idea. Alpine skiing is a classic example, based on very simple principles, but only introduced to the Alps in the last century. Recognising the importance of imagination in adventure, they decided to start a Dangerous Sports Club. The Club would be dedicated to creating new sports – or at least, taking a new approach to existing ones. They had no idea, at that time, whether they would succeed in being innovators, but they had at least made the vital commitment to try.

The following year saw them back in Switzerland to experiment with white water canoeing. Although not a brand new sport of their own, it had the merit of being something none of them had done before, or knew anything about. Approaching a sport without the knowledge of what is impossible should, they believed, free them from the mental shackles which limit the more experienced. There happened to be a world championship competition course on the river Landquart, conveniently close to some friends in Klosters, so they set out to try their luck.

Over the years, beginners' luck proved to be a faithful companion of the Club, and a collective attitude developed that it was better not to allow practice (or, worst of all, professional instruction), to interfere with intuition and natural, instinctive responses. After all, training, using systematic repetition, eliminates novelty and replaces natural reactions with learned ones. Instruction, a professionally-guided process of advancing in small, cautious steps, can turn an interesting experience into a pitifully tedious one, substituting cost for excitement. And all for competitive advantage – but at what a price!

One by one, they launched their canoes into the swollen, freezing river. In fact, only Chris had sufficient sense of balance to get a canoe down the course. Ed and David fell victim to the first whirling vortex, to the amusement of the local spectators, coming out half-drowned and ready for a stiff drink.

The Club, at this stage no more than an informal group of friends, expanded steadily, drawing on the unique human resource of Oxford University. Oxford gathers young, creative, and intellectual people from Britain and around the world, and puts them together in one of the most beautiful cities in Europe. Human nature being what it is, many of them enjoy their three years of intellectual and aesthetic stimulation, and end up with aspirations no higher than a career as a merchant banker, chartered accountant or computer engineer. However, some go on to make original contributions in their chosen fields, or at least seek to provoke rather than placate with their ideas. Such people were natural recruits to the new Club. A pushy student called Philip Oppenheim, another privileged young man, was among the early enthusiasts. However, the new Club was also attracting people from outside England's fossilised class structure, including those from the scientific side of the cultural divide.

Alan Weston, a hang-glider enthusiast recently arrived from Australia, was studying engineering. His eager smile and unmistakeable enthusiasm, together with his boyish good looks, excused the extremes of practical experimentation to which his vigour and curiosity led him. While in Australia, he had attempted strapping model aircraft engines to his back, hoping to become the first powered hang-glider pilot. The flight was not a success, but the damage was limited to the aircraft rather than the pilot. Escaping serious injury left his curiosity as well as his legs intact, and at Oxford's Engineering department he was able to take an increasingly well-organised approach to implementing his mechanical fantasies. The noise generated by his propeller-thrust measurement device attracted the attention of the like-minded as well as the irritated. Thus, he naturally gravitated to the Club, along with his fellow engineer, Crispin Balfour; but while Alan got seriously involved in the Club, Crispin did not. Still years away from being defined by anything more than occasional participation in absurd sporting and social activities, the Club attracted some who dipped a toe in the water and then moved on elsewhere, and others who plunged in with gusto and carry the effects for life.

When Ed and David decided to hold a cocktail party in the most remote place possible, the vagueness of Club membership made it difficult to guess how many would get involved, at least until some kind of effort was called for. David was always inclined to err on the side of excess, so, in the summer of 1978, he sent out over two hundred invitations to a cocktail party on Rockall. An isolated lump of granite in the North Atlantic, Rockall is claimed by Britain, partly from habit, but mainly so that the sea around it can be kept clear of foreign fishermen. Amazingly enough, very few of those invited decided to attend the party.

Alan set off with David, Ed, Chris, Crispin, and four other friends, together with skipper Mike Villiers-Stewart, in a small boat, heavily loaded with food and drink. The Atlantic weather was particularly bad. After a couple of days heaving and churning in the waves, the boat sprang a leak. It was dark at the time, and for a while nobody noticed that water was slowly filling the cabin. It was waist deep before someone started baling with a bucket. After a while, they found the water was coming in through a small drainage hole. Alan slowly realised that he was two hundred miles out to sea in a leaking boat, and somewhere in the back of his mind was the fact that, as on the Titanic, there were more people on the boat than spaces in the dinghy.

In his own words: *Alan Weston*

When we got to the end of the Crinan Canal, the weather had deteriorated to the point that we had a force nine gale, and a lot of the weekend sailors from Glasgow – suburbanites wearing their yellow bootees – who had gathered along the edge of the Canal when we set off, were muttering that we were all going to die. We didn't realise how bad it was going to be, only Mike Villiers-Stewart realised, but he was determined enough that he thought we could make it in his boat. There were so many people crowded on the boat that we had to have some people on deck all the time. It was extraordinarily rough.

At first it was so bad it was almost funny. It was the ultimate bad experience, being out in the middle of the ocean in a small boat in a gale. But then it just got worse and worse, until it wasn't funny any more. Everyone got seasick. I threw up just when Mike was downwind and he got a beard full of it, but he was too sick to even care. It was really, really bad. I went downstairs and lay down to die. I just lost interest in what was going on.

Then the bung came out and the boat started to fill with water. Most of us were too sick to care or to do anything about it. Fortunately there was one guy, a real hearty bugger who kept singing sea shanties, who had his shit together and realised that something needed to be done. He cracked open a bottle of champagne and carved the cork into a shape that he could stick in the hole. I wasn't taking much in then, I was just thinking how nice it would be to die and get it all over with. He saved our lives, basically. Later on, it calmed down and we began to feel better.

After five days, they found Rockall, and got into the boat's dinghy to approach it. The steep sides of the island rise straight out of the water. The dinghy was cramped and fragile, and they had to manoeuvre it close to the rock, so that one of them could jump on to it. The swell raised them close enough for David to jump on to the island, and climb to a point where he could attach a line. Once a few people were on the rock, they could haul up the supplies. They celebrated all day with scrambled eggs, dancing and champagne, leaving the eggshells and empties in the light beacon the Royal Navy had erected in 1972. In the spirit of good-natured vandalism which often accompanied the Club, they unscrewed the plaque attached to the beacon, proclaiming Rockall to be British territory, and kept it as a souvenir. They replaced it with a sign declaring the beacon to be a disabled persons' toilet.

*

The Club were probably the only people ever to visit Rockall for its own sake, rather than to raise a flag on it. In a crowded country such as Britain, any really good party will attract complaints and be stopped by the police. Finding a part of Britain which was hundreds of miles from the nearest uniformed official, yellow line, or bank manager was part of the fun; to be where the only real laws are those of nature, and petty, man-made rules do not apply. Curiously, in the late 1980s a man called John Ridgway went to Rockall and lived there for a week. I believe he held the record at the time for rowing the smallest boat across the Atlantic. He was a keen flag-waver, who no doubt affixed a further plaque declaring this deserted spot to be forever British. Most remarkably, he took sophisticated communications equipment with him so he could talk to his family every day. We may only wonder why he went to such an isolated place at all, if he was such a dedicated conversationalist. A good deal of publicity surrounded his venture, giving the impression that this particular kind of irrational behaviour is an admirable thing if done in a properly serious, nationalistic way.

There was nothing very serious about the Dangerous Sports Club's trip to Rockall. When the party wound down and the dinghy ferried revellers back to the boat, the last two on the island, Chris and David, ran over the 70-foot high cliff and into the sea.

3.

Flying Visits

*'We don't tackle flying through rock until a little
later in the programme.'*
– Richard Bach, *Jonathan Livingstone Seagull*

Alan Weston's first sporting love, hang-gliding, was a passion he shared with several other members of the Club. The level of experience may have varied between individuals, but they didn't care; a pilot's instincts and confidence are more important than mere flying hours, and are certainly more important than paper qualifications. This attitude took the Club to extraordinary feats of mountain flying and, along the way, on to the cinema screen.

When he graduated from Oxford in 1978, Alan made plans to drive to Austria, where the world hang-gliding championships were taking place, and from there to Greece. He suggested that his fellow Club members should join him there, and they would then fly hang-gliders off Mount Olympus. David and Chris took him up on the offer, both keen to attempt a really big mountain flight. They were also ironically amused at the torch-lighting role of Mount Olympus in the rule-infested, dollar-driven, flag-waving circus of the Olympic Games, where international hatred is carefully organised and everything is so predictable that tiny margins are considered crucial.

Alan drove out, together with his college friend Dave Turnbull, in a composite car which he had assembled from the parts of two old Rovers. (Dave, who had done no flying, and was not entirely convinced it was a good idea to learn hang-gliding at such demanding sites, was not planning to fly). They got to the hang-gliding competition in Austria, where Alan, although not a competitor, hoped to gain experience and learn from the techniques of the world's best. The competition site promised challenging flying conditions, and Alan watched the progress of other pilots as he assembled his kite. His eagerness soon turned to disappointment as he stalled on take-off and crashed into a tree. Alan and the car, which had also been crashed in Austria, were both looking a bit rough by the time they reached Athens to meet David and Chris.

The summit of Mount Olympus, once the home of the ancient Gods, is today a busy tourist attraction, crowded with energetic young hikers. Hiring mules to carry the hang-gliders, Alan, Dave, Chris and David climbed the 9,000-feet to the top, where, among the sightseers, they found a group of Americans who believed that the mythical Olympian Gods were actually aliens. They were surveying the mountain with delicate instruments in the hope of locating the remains of a UFO.

Alan chose a launch site. It was a ledge which stood over a precipitous drop, offering an exciting take-off. They left the hang-gliders there and retired to a mountain hut for the night. Overnight, the weather turned bad and all four were stuck in the hut for some days. When the weather finally improved, they found that Chris' hang-glider had been blown downhill and badly broken. Chris, who is not usually inclined to express strong emotions, was so upset he wanted to throw the hang-glider over the cliff, but Alan persuaded him to take it home and get it mended.

Moving right up to the edge, Alan put on his harness and clipped himself on to his machine. The wind was blowing up the cliff, and the others had to hold his wings down while he got ready. When the time came, he asked them to let him go, and immediately he shot straight up. A minute or two later an equally powerful down-draught threw him down again; this was real flying! A hang-glider is as elegant and free, once in the air, as it is awkward and constrained when folded up and tied to a car roof. Similarly, the pilot in flight has the freedom of the sky, limited only by gravity and aerodynamics, while before launch he is burdened and restricted by the machine and harness. The moment of take-off marks the change from awkward to elegant, from burdened to free, and against the backdrop of a beautiful mountain it is a moment of almost mystical spiritual uplift.

Alan had to fly his hang-glider at its top speed to avoid being blown back over the top of the mountain and into the dangerous turbulence downwind of it, where he would be smashed into the hillside. He pulled the control bar back until the wind screamed in the wires and scoured tears from his eyes. Slowly, he was winning his contest with the elements.

These small wings and the people who cling to them are like straws in the winds that blow around great mountains, but they are straws which have some choice in where they are blown, and only the Gods could have a better view of their mountain.

David waited for a long time, watching this eventful flight unfold, knowing that Alan had the fastest hang-glider. He would have to wait for the wind to drop before flying. David always had just enough instinct for self-preservation to draw back from the outright suicidal and reserve his courage for the merely foolhardy. He was not afraid to make what would be only his fifth hang-glider flight, from a cliff which experts would think twice about; he was irrational enough to trust his instincts and luck to see him through. He was, though, sufficiently rational to know that the flight could not be accomplished if the wind was faster than the top speed of his hang-glider. His lack of experience was a limit within himself, which he could transcend if he chose; the wind speed was a real, concrete limit which no amount of positive attitude could overcome. Recognising the difference between the unwise and the impossible, and judging this balance of irrationality, is a vital survival skill in the Real World; the wind is merciless to those who ignore its strength.

After a couple of hours, the wind became more gentle, and David made his leap over the edge. His flight was less controlled than Alan's, because he found himself struggling to correct a tendency for his hang-glider to turn left. He was unaware of this problem because he had previously decided not to take the trouble – or the risk – of making a test flight. David had a theory that each pilot has a certain number of good flights and a certain number of bad flights, and he didn't want to use up his good flights practising. Unable to steer into the up-currents of air, he could not soar properly and the flight took only half an hour. Even so, by the end of it his arms were exhausted from the strain of countering the left turn. However, he managed to get down to the same field as Alan, crash-landing in his accustomed fashion. Alan had already found a local supply of ouzo, and David joined him.

Dave Turnbull and Chris drove around the area until they

found the two pilots, and drove back to Athens, where the car's engine seized up. It was the end of the road for the composite Rover. Fortunately Alan still had one day's AA membership left, so the AA flew him and Dave Turnbull back home. The final score was two hang-glider flights, two damaged hang-gliders, substantial bar bills and one wrecked car. Over the years, this turned out to be a good deal better than average for a Dangerous Sports Club flying expedition. There was another outcome for Alan, who met his future ex-wife while in Greece.

The expedition to Olympus was only the beginning of the Club's career in expedition hang-gliding. Olympus was a strictly amateur affair, in which everyone paid their own way; but David believed the Club had significant commercial potential, and later ventures were carried out with a view to making money. He organised a bigger expedition the following year, to fly hang-gliders off Mount Kilimanjaro, in Tanzania, which is Africa's highest peak. This proved a much more difficult project, involving many unknown problems.

David made a deal with film producer and adventurer Julian Grant to make a TV movie of the expedition. Julian, who persuaded former international Rugby player Cliff Morgan of the BBC, to part with £15,000 to help finance the production, also raised money privately from his personal contacts. His plan was to produce a fifty-minute film which, after airing on the BBC, could be sold worldwide at a profit, with 25% going to the Club.

The production costs would be substantial, with travel for Club members and film crew, hotel bills, local porters and so on. Among the Club members on the expedition were David, Chris, Alan and newer members Simon Keeling, John and Jerome Fack, and Ashley Doubtfire. Simon, a research scientist, had respectable credentials as a Club pilot, i.e. almost no experience. The Fack twins, though, were both very experienced, and Ashley was actually a qualified hang-gliding instructor. Unofficially, he was regarded as the most expert pilot and the others would look to him if they faced a difficult decision. He was not, though, expected to train the less experienced fliers, who trusted to beginners' luck in keeping with the Club tradition.

Once the expedition arrived in Kenya, bureaucratic problems began to upset the loosely-planned schedule of events. The hang-glider pilots required permits for their flights, because there was a war going on nearby and the officials were nervous of any kind of aviation. African bureaucracy can try the patience of a saint, but the Club has always been short of saints and they sent David instead. Obtaining the permits took almost a week, involved spending more money, and left little time for the actual climbing and flying. Julian Grant planned to film the flights from a helicopter, which had its own schedule problems, and this put additional pressure on the expedition to climb Kilimanjaro as fast as possible.

Kilimanjaro, if taken slowly, is not a difficult climb. It is, though, 19,300-feet high, and the human body does not work properly at such altitudes until it has been allowed a few days to adjust. Because they climbed too quickly, the whole group were affected by headaches, nausea, fatigue and inability to think straight – classic hangover symptoms, in fact, but brought on by the thin mountain air. Only four of them reached the top in any condition to attempt a take-off. However, bureaucracy and altitude sickness were only the first hurdles the expedition faced. Those who had got to the top, now had to make a difficult launch and navigate to a safe landing area, crossing miles of dense forest in which a solitary hang-glider pilot could get permanently lost (and had done, the previous year). The Club pilots were not too worried about these hazards, though; a throbbing headache is pain enough, and anyway, given the chance to soar across the skies of Africa, having the freedom of all the space a man can see, who would waste time worrying about getting lost? After all, back when the map of Africa showed nothing but the shape of its coastline, Henry Morton Stanley had crossed the continent equipped with little more than a sound classical education and a stiff upper lip.

In his own words: *Julian Grant*

Off we went to Kilimanjaro with a team of four or five cameras, and a helicopter booked. We went first to Nairobi, and we had enormous problems getting into Tanzania. We had to fly into Tanzania, and I remember being met at the airport by Kirke and one other, and in the vehicle on the way to the hotel on the edge of Kilimanjaro, David and I started to argue over the production finance.

It was a most acrimonious time in the hotel and leading up to the climb, because nothing was organised. It was left to me and the film crew to organise everything and we were organising the film side as well. There were enormous problems. When we went out to test the take-off techniques and flying capabilities of Club members it was seriously frightening because, apart from the three experts, they couldn't fly. David Kirke was probably the best, but Simon Keeling was a disaster waiting to happen. We then found they had not organised any sort of porterage to the top of the mountain, so I organised the porters. The commissioner was terrified because they had lost a couple of hang-gliders somewhere in the jungle round Kilimanjaro the year before, but anyway we persuaded him...

One other incident that happened in pre-production was that I had a serious row with Philip Oppenheim. I found out that a couple of the Club intended to have sedan chairs made by the local carpenter, and they were going to hire black labour to carry them to the top of Kilimanjaro. In fact, I informed the porters that they could carry gear in these sedan chairs, but if any of the Club actually asked to be carried, they were to bring them into camera range and then tip them out.

Kirke and I had a very difficult relationship, but I still thought what he was doing was amazing.

Ashley Doubtfire put his hang-glider together and went first. He managed a good take-off and flew out over the sheet of clouds covering the trackless forest below the mountain. The sun shone very brightly on the cloud, and for a long time the hang-glider could be seen as a black speck against brilliant white. David opened a bottle of champagne and passed it around, more out of habit than thirst. Head spinning, he picked up his hang-glider and steadied himself for the launch. The top of the mountain was covered in small, loose stones, adding poor grip to the problems of taking off with the brain working at one-tenth normal speed, and the need to run faster than usual to take off in the thin air. He began his run and, managing to keep the hang-glider straight, was soon airborne and flying away from the mountain. Often, in later years, he would reflect on this flight, the one which he regarded as his most exhilarating. The freedom and solitude of the African sky stamped an impression on him which lasted long after the throbbing head and eyes were forgotten, leaving him with memories he could look back on years afterwards, whenever the everyday world offered nothing but hassle and difficulties.

The next to go was Simon Keeling. On his take-off run, he allowed the hang-glider to enter a turn, and once airborne he over-corrected it, leading to a wild, swinging flight which took him very close to crashing into a large boulder. Once clear of this hazard, he followed the first two on the long glide down. Finally, Alan, last of the four who had reached the top fit to go, picked up his machine and began to run down the hill. He took off, immediately stalled, and crashed straight into a pile of rocks.

'Are you all right?' asked the cameraman, Tony Browning, as soon as he had framed a good close-up of the bent, torn glider and its pilot. Fortunately, Alan was unhurt, and was able to sum up his disappointment:

'I packed the kite with a spear, a hunting knife for the jungle, I've got water on me, I've got survival rations, I've got flares, I've got everything I could possibly need to survive in the jungle for about a week. Unfortunately I've only got about thirty feet, which is a bit of a let-down really,' he said from the wreckage of his kite.

In his own words: *Alan Weston*

We jumped off from the rim – it's a volcano – which is not actually the highest point. There's a fairly reasonable take-off site – actually it's a bit dangerous, because there's a bloody great rock in the flight path, which Simon nearly piled into – but a feasible take-off site, at about 18,500-feet. At this altitude the air density is about half what it is at sea level, so you have to go 40% faster to take off, and because the air is so thin it's hard to walk, let alone run. Olympus was easier, because you had this long way to fall to build up speed. At Kilimanjaro, you had to get up to flying speed by running really hard.

Kirke did a really good run, he actually did the best take-off. It's all a question of commitment, of craziness – you have to run like crazy and not have any doubts in your mind that you're going to succeed. I did have doubts – you've got to run so hard it's very difficult to do, and that's why I crashed – because I wasn't able to build up sufficient speed, stalled on take-off and spun in.

Simon hadn't actually flown his glider before. It was a high-performance glider and very sensitive to pilot input, very touchy. He over-controlled like crazy, and just managed to miss this boulder. Even after he missed the boulder he kept on over-controlling. It was a severe pilot-induced oscillation.

Out of eight would-be flyers, three had flown successfully, one had crashed, one (Chris) had broken his glider in the foothills before the climb, one had given up through altitude sickness, and two had been unable to stay for the delayed climb. It was not a bad success rate. Nobody got married this time. However, Julian

Grant was none too happy. Poor communications with the flyers had prevented him filming their take-offs from the helicopter. Only one hang-glider, Simon's, had been fitted with a working camera. Even that had only yielded a few seconds of good film. Julian put together a rough edit of the planned fifty-minute TV film, but it was very short of good action footage, despite the considerable amount of money that had been spent. Julian had never quite understood his subjects, or been able to get on well with them. There was another consideration; David Kirke now insisted on including more, new events, expanding the scope of the film from a single expedition, to a whole sequence of activities. The film remained unfinished, and therefore unsold.

Therefore, those who had triumphed over African bureaucracy, climbed the mountain, beaten altitude sickness, and flown across the jungle, faced one last obstacle: the cost. The expedition was short of money to pay the travel agents, Abercrombie and Kent. About £17,000 short, in fact. As organiser of the expedition, David Kirke was the one who faced the creditors, a situation he was to become all too familiar with.

*

It was to be five more years before the Club mounted another high-altitude hang-gliding expedition. In the meantime, there were other avenues to explore and new sports to devise, which were about to take the Club into uncharted regions of the Real World, as well as bringing the attention of people around the globe to what they were doing.

4.

Urban Vine Jumping

'We stand upon the brink of a precipice. We peer into the abyss – we grow sick and dizzy. Our first impulse is to shrink from the danger. Unaccountably we remain.'
– Edgar Allan Poe

While David was busy organising the Kilimanjaro expedition, Chris Baker was working on an idea of his own, one which ultimately developed far beyond all expectations and is today the basis of a fast-growing worldwide industry – bungee jumping. When it was first attempted, and for some time afterwards, bungee jumping was widely regarded as tantamount to suicide. Nobody expected it to become a mass participation sport. It was left in the domain of the kind of person who appears to care neither for their safety nor their reputation; the kind that people of common sense call crazy. Yet it has been transformed from novelty, through stunt, to sport and even commercial fairground ride in just a few short years, a process which normally takes far longer, and it is today the most obvious legacy of the Dangerous Sports Club.

The fear of heights is a survival instinct bred into us ever since we came down from the trees and stood up on our hind legs, so the defiance of it arouses primordial bodily responses; sweat, tension, adrenaline. The act of casting the body down from a great height requires a triumph of intellect over instinct, and the flight that follows usually provokes wild laughter, screams of earthy words, and a grin that takes some time to fade away. Frequent jumps make it a familiar sensation, and it soon loses its potency, but for the first few times it has a powerful effect.

Often, the concept is attributed to the Pentecost islanders of the South Pacific, who are said to have rituals involving jumping from trees with vines tied to their legs. The vines tighten just before impact, slowing the jumper just enough to prevent fatal injury – usually. Some accounts describe this peculiar tradition as a test of manhood. Others relate an ancient legend about a woman who tricked her husband in a suicide pact by using a vine to save herself, while the husband plunged to his death, since which time all the men have had to learn the technique just in case. Whatever the origin of vine jumping may be, it offers no rebound or upward flight. The vines are not sufficiently elastic; they merely break the fall, in a bone-jarring but survivable way. Vine jumping is the sort of thing which schoolboys hear about as a curiosity, and if your mind works like Ed Hulton's, it stays in the back of your thoughts and resists the attempts of adult concerns to crowd it out. Soon after forming the Club, Ed had suggested a vine-jumping expedition to New Guinea, but the time and money involved meant the idea was quickly shelved, although not forgotten.

In the late-Seventies, Chris was living in Bristol, within sight of the great Clifton Suspension bridge, one of the many still-functioning engineering masterpieces of Isambard Kingdom Brunel. As a keen hang-glider pilot, Chris had a reel of elastic bungee cord, which he used to strap hang-gliders to his car roofrack. One day it dawned upon him that bungee cord could provide a way to vine-jump the bridge. The idea intrigued him, and he mentioned it to the other members of the Club. There were some predictable jokes about knicker elastic, and David, his mind already turning to practicalities, suggested using climbing harnesses to attach the jumper to the bungee. Chris was convinced it was an idea worth trying, and in early 1979 he set about arranging it.

Chris bought some of the thickest type of bungee rope available, the sort used for catapulting gliders into the air. He asked a mathematician friend to work out the length of bungee required for the jump, given the weight of the jumper and the elastic properties of the bungee rope. The theoretical answer was to use four parallel strands of the rope, tied together, and that the length should be half the height of the bridge, which is about 250 feet. Alan Weston checked this figure using a computer model of the proposed jump and agreed that it ought to work.

A more cautious individual might have carried out a test, using a suitable weight, before actually jumping. Chris, though, felt that the essence of the experience would be making a leap into the unknown, with the outcome admittedly predicted in theory, but still uncertain until actually attempted. He wanted to climb over the railing of the bridge and launch himself into an unknown region, not one already explored, even by sandbags.

Chris announced a date for the first jump; April Fools' Day, 1979. He would hold a party the night before, naturally, and many invitations were sent out. Chris had enough bungee rope for four jumpers, and had also obtained the necessary harnesses and attachments. The last day of March saw a large group assemble for the party, and they began to consume the many and various intoxicants provided. Chris, the host, drove to London to fetch his girl-friend.

Chris got back around dawn and saw the party-goers at the arranged meeting-point, a garage near the bridge. There was a delay; the police had been tipped off to expect some kind of stunt on the bridge, and were watching. David was impatient; he wanted to get on with the jump, partly for its own sake and partly because he had arranged for it to be filmed by Julian Grant. The jump would help to complete the film which had begun with the Kilimanjaro expedition.

Chris went home to change; as usual, wanting to be dressed ready for the undertaker. Walking back towards the bridge, he was startled to see first David Kirke, then Alan Weston, Simon Keeling, and finally Tim Hunt, jumping off the bridge. The idea that they would go ahead without him, however late he was, when the project had been his idea, had never crossed his mind. After all, he had paid for the bungee ropes, harnesses and party, which was no small expense. But he had missed the crucial moment when the police had given up, presuming the tip-off to be an April Fools' hoax, and left the bridge, creating an opportunity for the jump to go ahead.

In his own words: *Xan Rufus-Isaacs*

I remember the first bungee jump. There was a party at Chris Baker's flat in Clifton. I went there with Tim Hunt, and I remember magic mushrooms being provided to one and all. We were in the most terrible state, certainly by the next morning. It was a fairly squalid sort of party even by the usual standards, although I must say Chris had a nice flat. There were a lot of people being very ill. The first time I saw Clifton Bridge was when dawn came up that morning. Chris Baker had disappeared to London to pick up some girl, and everyone got kitted out in a garage just before the jump. I hid David in the back of my old Renault with all the ropes on his lap. I got on to the bridge and kicked David out of the Renault, and tied one end of the rope on to the bridge. Then he clambered over the railing and off he went. There was a tremendous amount of howling and screaming and celebrating, and then we saw he'd dropped the bottle of champagne and lost his hat.

There was very much the feeling that this was something sort of historic – it was an unbelievable sight. People were just scratching their heads in absolute bewilderment. I was looking down over the bridge when all the guys were jumping off, and Simon Keeling, cool as a goddam cucumber, just said, 'OK, guys, see you later,' and vaulted over. Hunt was hanging on by his fingertips, and then let go when the police were coming over the bridge to get him. He wasn't very happy, but he'd done a lot of mushrooms. There is a road at the bottom of Clifton Gorge, and I remember watching a car drive along it as various people jumped, and this car just lost it completely and literally skidded right round. Some bloke got out of it and he couldn't believe what was going on.

Although he was too late to make the first ever bungee jump himself, the idea worked just as Chris had first imagined it. The four jumpers fell freely until the rope began to stretch, then they were slowed down and eventually stopped. The tension in the bungee cords then shot them back up to within twenty feet of the bridge, and then they fell again, each time bouncing back a little less, until they came to rest suspended like puppets in the middle of the Avon gorge, laughing and waving.

In his own words: *Alan Weston*

I made a computer simulation of the jump, but we didn't do the obvious thing and test it – that was considered unsporting. Chris was in the process of breaking up with his girlfriend and in the middle of the party, he got called up, and disappeared to London. By the time he got back, his house had been completely destroyed. He came back to his house and I think he waited there, a bit shocked to find it in such a state, and basically he missed the jump by being late. I didn't even know he was back – it was unfortunate, as he had paid for it all. It was a really big party – he spent a fortune on booze.

David was the one who pushed for it to happen, whether Chris was there or not. Actually I didn't particularly want to jump – it was one of those things you talk about, but you don't think you're really going to do it. I was terrified. We were standing there on the edge of the bridge. David got ready first and he jumped. I was a coward – I watched him and saw that it worked, then thought, 'Oh fuck, I'm going to have to do it!' So I jumped second, about the same time as Simon.

A frustrated and confused squad of policemen arrived as the jumpers were being hauled back up by hand, a laborious process. The police didn't really know what to make of it, but they knew they didn't like it. Each jumper, as they were lifted back over the rail, was arrested and taken to the police station. No-one was quite sure what charges would be preferred, except perhaps that old standby, breach of the peace. They were kept in the cells overnight and appeared before magistrates the next day. The magistrates were unable to see the funny side of it, and the four jumpers were fined £100 each and bound over to keep the peace. The ropes were returned.

The press coverage was immense. Most national newspapers ran stories which were entirely sympathetic to the Club. The press had suddenly discovered the Club's existence, and found it a rich source of material. Not only did the bungee jumps make good photographs, the jumpers themselves, formal dress and all, did too. The connection with Oxford and the class symbols in the Club's style provided a ready-made stereotype which the press seized upon. David's willingness to provide quotable one-liners made him, in particular, an ideal subject for reporters. He was not averse to the attention, and over the years, many journalists have written feature articles about him.

An example of his quotable, snappy style is the following, unrehearsed, film interview by Julian Grant, an hour before the jumps were made:

Julian: 'David, can you tell me what the Dangerous Sports Club is, exactly?'

David: 'Um, it's just a collection of people who are quite unacceptable in any other terms.'

Julian: 'What's your aim in life?'

David: 'Our aim is to avoid everybody who has an aim.'

Julian: 'Is money involved in this stunt you're about to pull today?'

David: 'Um, debts are involved, but debts don't count as money.'

Julian: 'But you're not doing this for any financial reward?'

David: 'Er, we wouldn't know what finance is, still less a reward.'

Despite the revealing remark about his attitude to debts, David was being a little evasive in his last reply; apart from having an interest in the film Julian was making, he had also made an arrangement with the *Daily Mail*, providing them with advance warning of the event. Under a half-page picture of the jump, they printed a story about the Club which mentioned other exploits such as the party on Rockall, and the hang-gliding expedition to Kilimanjaro. The four jumpers were all named, starting with Tim Hunt because his brother was a famous racing driver, a connection all the newspapers had focused on. The article continued: 'David Kirke (33), a university lecturer, said, "People may think we are mad. We think they are insane to endure such humdrum lives."' The patronising tone of this remark did not spoil the favourable overall impression left by the coverage, which continued with an appearance on the *Nationwide* early evening BBC TV show.

Jumping in top hats and tailcoats was one of the details the Club had decided on without much consideration; it seemed obvious, somehow natural. It turned out to be a powerful image-building move, which reporters and cameramen always relished. It became the instant trademark of the Club, and lent an air of 'Dr Livingstone, I presume?' formality to otherwise ridiculous behaviour. No doubt Isambard Kingdom Brunel, himself a top hat wearer, would have approved.

The success of the world's first bungee jumps proved the concept of using elastic rope in this way, and it became obvious that structures all over the world were just begging to be jumped. Indeed, David was quoted as saying, 'We want to start a craze, like streaking.' This did not happen straight away, but today, almost every high bridge in the world has been bungee-jumped. The elegance and simplicity of the idea struck a chord around the globe, ultimately inspiring millions to do likewise. However, for a few years yet, the Dangerous Sports Club had their brand new sport all to themselves.

The next bungee jump was at the Golden Gate bridge in San Francisco in October 1979. On the way out, David, Chris and Ed, the original founders of the Club, visited the island of St Vincent in the Caribbean, where a volcano was erupting – always a fascinating event to them. A rumour reached them that a Sunderland flying boat was moored on a nearby island, and was for sale. They went to look.

When they entered the giant hangar, they found not one, but two of the magnificent four-engined aircraft. These giant white machines had been built by Short Brothers of Northern Ireland and used by the Navy during World War II. David, Ed and Chris, all flying enthusiasts, felt a sense of awe on beholding these great woolly mammoths of the air. Ed, the richest by a considerable margin, felt sufficiently moved to reach for his wallet and buy one of them, for about £70,000. Restoring the Sunderland to flying condition occupied him for the next few years, and the expense of the work and the subsequent operating costs almost broke him. Such was the expense that Ed had a white elephant insignia painted on the tail fin. Having acquired a new interest in life, Ed took no further active role in the Club.

Chris and David moved on to San Francisco, meeting with the other jumpers, Alan Weston, Simon Keeling, Peter Carew and Janie Wilmot. They made a well-publicised bungee jump from the Golden Gate bridge which went fairly smoothly, except for Chris getting his rope tangled in the structure of the bridge, preventing his jump. Alan and Simon abseiled down to a getaway boat, and escaped arrest, but the others were booked for trespass. After spending over a thousand dollars on a lawyer, they were given $10 fines.

The publicity surrounding the jump, which was the first in America, was huge. In America, huge publicity means money, and it led to an offer David could not refuse from a TV company who were making a show called *That's Incredible*. The producer, Alan Landsberg, offered $20,000 to film a bungee jump from the Royal Gorge Bridge in Colorado, the highest bridge in the world. It is a suspension bridge, just over 1,000-feet high. The Club obliged with five simultaneous jumps, Clifton style.

Club members drove from San Francisco to the bridge site in Colorado in a cavalcade of borrowed or hired cars, each of them groaning under the weight of people and drink. At the bridge, they found that Alan Landsberg was taking things suitably seriously, hiring a helicopter to capture the most dramatic possible angles. He was expecting to be able to film the jumps the next morning and then leave, but the Club had more elaborate preparations in mind, considering the event a celebration to be savoured, rather than a job to be quickly and efficiently executed. To begin with, they had to find a piano for Hubie Gibbs, the Club pianist, before considering any jumping. The film crew tolerated the leisurely pace of events, though, realising that this was the only way the Club knew how to do it.

Along with David Kirke, Alan Weston and Tim Hunt, three of the original four Clifton jumpers, two new jumpers took part, Paul Foulon and Geoff Tabin. Paul was a relative of Alan, and Geoff was a mountaineer who applied his expertise with ropes to the technical aspects of the jump. Neither of them went on to become Club regulars, and Geoff later disgraced himself in David's eyes by writing a story about the jump, which included an inaccurate, potted biography of David himself, for *Playboy* magazine. David, by this time, appreciated the value of publicity and wanted to control it himself.

The bungee ropes were of various lengths, and the longest was David's, at 420-feet. No-one had ever used such long ropes before, and the mathematical estimates of their elasticity were very uncertain. By this time, nobody cared to work things out in too much detail any more; bungee jumping was now known to be survivable, so all that remained was to get on with it. The TV crew had scheduled the jump for 8am, when the wind would be light, but this failed to allow for hangovers, and the jumpers were not ready until 3pm. The cameramen were not the only ones who wanted to get on with the action; Alan was becoming impatient too. He found the jump intimidating enough, but the presence of a Mormon choir at one end of the bridge, singing praises for his deliverance, was irritating him.

Finally, in the late afternoon, all five jumpers, well fortified with champagne and wearing the now-obligatory top hat and tails, stepped over the rail and plummeted into the Gorge. The TV crew breathed a sigh of relief; some of them had doubted that these well-dressed revellers were actually going to deliver the goods at all, but the spectacle was up to their highest expectations and well worth the waiting and worrying. The film was broadcast many times in the USA and also abroad. Although the jumps were spectacular, the practical difficulties of recovering the jumpers were greater than anyone had realised. The method used before was hauling back up by manpower, but with the considerable extra weight of rope, and strong wind pressure on the five men, it proved a much longer task than before. David, the last to be retrieved, was left hanging for hours and grew bitterly cold in the wind. The leg straps of the harness, which supported most of his body weight, became very uncomfortable, and eventually cut off the circulation in his legs. By the time he got back to the top, he was suffering mild hypothermia, which muted his enthusiasm. He had also discovered that very long bungee ropes provide a disappointing bounce; the sensation is of sinking down gently and coming to rest, rather than flying vigorously back up.

The trip to Colorado was an orgy of spending, and by the time the Club left, every cent of the $20,000 had gone. A fundamental weakness in the financial prospects of the Club was becoming apparent; the ability of Club members to spend money was limitless. David in particular had a weakness for extravagance, preferably at someone else's expense, but failing that, at his own. However much money there was, it would all be spent, and then some.

Following the jumps in the USA, David, alone of the three founders of the Club, returned to England. Ed's attention was devoted to his Sunderland flying boat, and Chris remained in the USA for four years, developing and selling hang-gliders. David now assumed complete control of the Club and its activities, becoming the proprietor of the Club as a commercial enterprise. He had long since given up trying to hold down an ordinary job, and decided to make the Club his full time occupation. His next project involved powered hang-gliders.

Various experimental and very dodgy powered hang-gliders had begun to appear in the late-Seventies. These aircraft, or at least their descendants, today known as microlights, are now considered sensible aircraft. In 1980, though, sensible was not a word many people were using to describe them.

David decided to fly one across the Channel to Paris in the summer of 1980. David has always attached a special significance to the English Channel, and whenever I saw him encounter a new mode of transport, I knew one of the first things he would want to do with it was cross the Channel. The crossing by powered hang-glider was to be covered once again by the press, who would contribute financially. Newspapers are supposed to report the news rather than create it, but reporters are often willing to offer cash, on the pretence that the event is happening anyway (and is therefore a news item rather than a paid performance), and that they are just paying for information about the time and place. A few hundred pounds is about the best a national daily will offer. (If the event is illegal, they are quite prepared to tip off the police so they can photograph your arrest as well, which often gives them their best pictures).

David arranged for a trial flight in the grounds of Longleat House. After flying around one of England's stateliest homes, he was filled with enthusiasm for the Channel flight. The first attempt, though, did not get far. Three machines took off, with a motor boat standing by to cover the sea crossing, and a helicopter available for press photographers. Julian Grant was also there to film the event, hoping at last to finish his TV programme. However, the improvised fuel tanks shifted in flight, making the aircraft unbalanced and liable to stall repeatedly. All three made forced landings, and no-one reached the English coast.

On the second attempt, David, flying alone this time, and without such fanfare, got all the way to Paris, violating controlled airspace for his first time, and landed in a field outside the city. The farmer had been a Resistance worker in wartime, and it reminded her of the old days to once more to have as her guest an English aviator on the run . David, heartened by the successful flight and refreshed by her hospitality, returned to Oxford in good spirits. The Club – his business – was going strong.

David called Julian Grant and announced his success. Julian, exasperated, told him it was no use making a successful flight if it was not filmed, at least not from his point of view, and no, he did not want to film a third attempt. The film project had become a shambles, with a series of events, none of which were properly filmed, some of them recorded only by still pictures, and with no money left for editing and other post-production costs. Julian himself was about £20,000 down on the venture. His business instincts screamed at him to cut his losses and abandon the project.

The film was eventually finished by another producer, Patrick Gamble. The finished movie included Julian Grant's Kilimanjaro and Clifton footage. By arrangement with Alan Landsberg, it also had shots of the Golden Gate and Colorado bungee jumps, and there was film of the first, unsuccessful Channel crossing attempt. These sections were edited together with interview material, scenic film of Oxford, and even some still pictures, a technique not usually considered acceptable in movies. Even with such padding material, the final version was barely 45 minutes long. It was released in the cinema as a supporting feature in early 1981, under the title, *The History of the Dangerous Sports Club*. It was never, after all, shown on TV.

The film actually did very well, if only because it was the supporting feature of a film called *Private Lessons*, starring Sylvia Kristel, whose charms presumably put most of the bums on the cinema seats. It was the eighth biggest-grossing British film of 1982, and the only short film in the chart; although it was only the distributors who made money out of the success, because they had linked it to a mainstream A-feature.

*

Vine-jumping folklore about the natives of the Pentecost Islands, Vanuatu, or Papua New Guinea (depending who is telling the story), turns out to be difficult to substantiate. There is no record, among the detailed journals kept by Victorian missionaries, of any vine jumping in the last century. The suicide pact legend is actually a variation on an ancient religious story, which has nothing to do with vine jumping. The first verified, eyewitness account of vine jumping is post-war, and comes from an island on which the US had an air base during the war. There was a parachute training tower at this base, from which aircrew used to jump, suspended by ropes. So, perhaps the idea is really not so old after all.

Ed Hulton did, eventually, finish restoring the flying boat. Securing the services of the last active pilot still qualified to fly a Sunderland, he brought it to England, and had the pleasure of landing in it on the Thames near Tower Bridge. Sadly, though, it had cost so much that in 1992 he had to sell it to an American collector.

5.

The Northern Chemist

'It's grim up North.'
– The KLF

In the autumn of 1980, I arrived in Oxford to study physics. I was a spotty, unremarkable eighteen-year-old who had just left an unpretentious comprehensive school, nervously clutching my A-levels. From a distance, Oxford University had seemed an institution designed to exclude people like me – an elitist place for those already on top of the heap. However, over the years it has progressively opened its doors ever wider, and when my time came, it made me welcome. Like much of Britain, it still carries the trappings of a grand history, and while doing what it must to keep abreast of modern developments, it retains many of the peculiarities that have accumulated over the centuries, which make Oxford distinct and interesting.

Oxford is an arts-dominated University, and I heard much disparaging talk of science students, generally labelling them as dull bookworms. In fact, the commonest way of describing someone boring was to call them a Northern Chemist, rolling regional and intellectual prejudices into one. It was not necessary to be either Northern or a Chemistry student to be considered a Northern Chemist (I was neither); it was more a state of being. However, I hoped not to spend all my time at Oxford in libraries, labs and lectures, becoming a science bore. As I carried my bag from the station to my college, I was looking forward to the renowned pleasures of Oxford Student Life.

It took me some time to adjust to the hothouse atmosphere of life in the ancient university. Each year's work is compressed into three terms of just eight weeks. This short time is filled with intense activity – social, sporting, political, artistic, musical, sexual and literary – as well as academic work. Lecture attendance is voluntary, and students are not unduly limited by the distraction of fixed timetables – a precious freedom.

There are a bewildering variety of University clubs and societies, including large, well-funded clubs for the mainstream activities such as politics, drama, the more popular sports, and so on. Smaller clubs, for those with more obscure interests, also flourish. Then, there are a number of clubs whose appeal is based solely on social events, loud music, drinking to excess, promiscuity, and other such things of interest to teenagers. At the beginning of each academic year, the clubs all set out their stalls at the Freshers' Fair, in the hope of attracting new members. I walked around the Fair, spoilt for choice of clubs to join. However, although I had heard of the Dangerous Sports Club, and knew it was somehow connected with Oxford, I realised that it would not have a stall at the Fair. To start with, although it was often described as an Oxford Club, it seemed unlikely that it actually enjoyed any formal link with the University. Nor did I imagine that such a Club really wanted to attract an acne-ridden horde of teenage Northern Chemists into its ranks. The public image of the Club suggested that its recruitment methods would be less formal and more discriminating. Besides, at that time I had no idea that I wanted to join it. When I went to the Fair, I was actually looking for the sort of clubs in which I could have a good time and meet people (female people in particular), without spending too much money or, for that matter, risking my neck.

I joined a couple of such clubs, and was about to leave, when I saw the stall of the Parachute Club. I felt a cartoon light bulb flash on above my head. Until I saw this stall, I didn't know that parachuting was available to normal people as an ordinary sport. The only people I'd heard of doing free-fall parachute jumps were soldiers, or TV action men like John Noakes. In one of those *Aha!* moments, it struck me that this was the only club I really wanted to join, even though I guessed straight away that parachuting was going to prove expensive (which it was), and that small, remote airfields were not the best places to meet girls (which they aren't).

Not much later, I spent a cold Saturday morning at a just such a small, remote airfield, along with about thirty others, learning how to climb out of the tiny cabin of a light aircraft, and dangle from the wingstrut until the instructor shouted at us to let go. We were then supposed to count to four in a loud voice, and look up to see if our blind faith in silk and string was justified. If not, we were to open the reserve parachute, which in those days was still carried on the belly. We practiced landing by jumping off a stool and rolling over in a patch of gravel, which was liberally sprinkled with sheep-shit. On the next day, Sunday, we were ready to jump for real.

I was the last of a plane-load of three first-timers, and watched with fascination while the other two stepped out, clinging to the wingstrut, and then disappeared from sight, leaving their static lines banging against the side of the plane. We circled round again, the instructor told me to climb out, and I hung on to the strut with the cold wind screaming in my ears. Looking back into the small plane, and seeing the instructor's face framed in the aircraft door, I had the strange sensation of being alongside it, as if flying in formation with the plane instead of clinging to it with white fingers. The instructor shouted, 'Go!', and as I let go and fell away, I had a cast-iron certainty of my own to add to those of ground and gravity; I knew that I would be back for more.

With teenage enthusiasm, I soon started spending all my weekends and money on jumping, and before long I found myself organising the University Parachute Club. Much as I was interested in my studies, and enjoying student life, I could hardly wait to leave Oxford and go parachuting at weekends. So, most Saturdays, I would get up before dawn and hitch-hike forty miles north towards Stratford-upon-Avon, where there was an old wartime airfield used for parachuting.

As a beginner, I used a traditional, round parachute, with a static line to pull it open as I fell from the plane. The static line is a very reliable device, needing no skill, but offering little challenge, so my first target was the point at which I could make free-fall jumps. I didn't feel I was a real skydiver until I was pulling my own ripcord. After reaching that landmark, the student parachutist had a whole sequence of other skills to learn, and as you progressed, you jumped from higher altitudes, making longer free falls, until you finally finished your training and were considered a competent skydiver. At this point you could jump with a high-performance square parachute, and you could do something called Relative Work. This is a clumsy name for something so beautiful. RW means jumping with your friends and making formations with your bodies while falling. If you all fall at the same speed, you appear simply to float around each other, and can move anywhere you want relative to your friends.

If you have ever dreamed, like me, of being able to fly as if by magic, this is the nearest it is possible to get. I had never known a more sensual or inspiring experience than RW; it never failed to stir me inside and leave me hungry for more.

Of course, before long you run out of magic and have to open a parachute. To hardcore RW jumpers, though, the free-fall is the only important part of the jump. The parachute is just a brake which stops you hitting the ground too hard, and the canopy ride is a sort of rehabilitation to everyday, earthbound life, after the fun of RW. By the time you reach this state of mind, skydiving ceases to be a dare or a thrill; it is familiar territory, an arena in which to play, perform, compete, and develop skills. Regular jumpers can become obsessive, making remarks about everyday life seeming to be no more than a way of passing the time between jumps. People who have newly discovered an enthusiasm for skydiving often have an overwhelming urge to re-organise their lives so they can do more jumping. Such is the joy of liberation from society's risk-taboo; the delight of taking the first steps outside the cage it puts around us, and making weekend forays into the real world outside. The same effect happens to those who take up climbing, potholing, sailing, diving and so on; it just happened that with me, it was RW skydiving.

People doing RW were easy to spot; they wore ridiculously baggy, brightly coloured jumpsuits (jumpsuit design was stuck firmly in the early-Seventies), and they kept doing little rain dances, bent over at the waist, rehearsing their next sequence of formations; this was called 'dirt diving'. These experienced jumpers were a friendly bunch, and held good parties.

I organised a series of first-jump courses for other University students, and I was genuinely surprised that 98% of people who joined the club, did one jump only and then never returned (at that time I was a poor judge of human nature). Almost all of them said what a terrific experience it was, but for some obscure reason, they could not be persuaded to do it again. I didn't understand. What was wrong with these people?

I worked steadily through the training system, but found it frustratingly slow, largely because it was so often too cloudy or windy to jump. I spent many days at the airfield waiting for the weather to improve – not a rewarding pastime in Britain. It took months to learn the basics, and I felt I would never reach the stage at which I could do RW. In the end, responding to the urge for more and better jumping, I re-organised my life by spending the summer of 1981 working in an American travelling carnival, so that I could jump in the Californian sunshine; and there, at last, I learned the magical art of dancing in the sky.

*

In early 1981, a fellow physics student called Henry Robinson, one of the handful of first-time parachutists who did more than one jump, introduced me to David Kirke, who at the time was interested in doing a parachute course. We met in the Bear, a popular but cramped pub behind Christ Church, Henry's college. David was living in North Oxford, in a room so filled with books, rubbish and strange equipment that it was quite difficult to get through the door. I had seen pictures of him bungee jumping in a top hat and tailcoat, but the clothes he wore on a day to day basis gave him an air of shabbiness. Clearly, like me, he normally hung up his clothes on the floor, but, unlike mine, some of his clothes had once been smart and expensive. He was thirty-six, but looked well over forty. He had the air of a slightly distracted, pipe-smoking, middle-aged philosophy don, and over the years he seldom bothered to deny the frequent, but incorrect, press reports that he was just that.

I met others who frequented the Bear, and found that my experience was not unusual:

In his own words: *Xan Rufus-Isaacs*

I first met David in the Bear in my second year at Oxford, and I remember many long, drunken afternoons at Park Town [David's address]. We had a regular Wednesday afternoon tequila session. It was then one started hearing rather odd stories about these flying machines, and meeting people such as Alan Weston. I remember David's room in Park Town. There were books everywhere. We were in a city of books, and I had never seen so many books in one room. And then there were harnesses and pictures of odd machines.

After a few pints in the Bear, I expressed an interest in doing some bungee jumping, and before long I was asked to lend a hand at a bungee jump just outside Oxford, in which, for the first time, the jump platform was to be an aircraft; a hot-air balloon, to be precise. The balloon was tethered by two ropes tied down to cars, with small height adjustments to be made on a third rope, until the balloon was at the desired altitude. This was measured in the most direct way possible, by hanging a 200ft string from the basket. The end was weighted with a sword, and I was given the task of controlling the tether rope so that the sword hung just off the ground. Discarding the 200ft string, David could then jump, knowing that he had enough clearance under him and would not hit the ground. He was making the jump for the benefit of the London Weekend TV show, *Game For A Laugh*. The jump went entirely to plan except in one respect; the pilot of the balloon, unsure as to whether this sort of thing was any good for his balloon, or for his continued possession of a pilot's licence, declined to take up any other jumpers. We had hoped to be allowed three or four jumps, but the balloon was landed and deflated as soon as it was clear that the film of the first jump was satisfactory. I was going to have to wait a little longer for my first bungee jump.

To make up for the disappointment, we went to one of Oxford's better restaurants, which had an up-and-coming young chef called Raymond Blanc. We had a fine hors d'oeuvres, a beautifully presented main course accompanied by a wine far too good for me to appreciate, followed by crème caramel with cognac. This was my first experience of serious lunching with David; the bill was picked up by London Weekend TV. I was on the learning curve.

The learning process resumed next time I met David in the Bear, when he appeared preoccupied with a £200 fine for some motoring offence, which he was required to pay by the end of the week. As it was early in the term and I still had some of my grant left, I was persuaded to assist David with his fine, but I was sufficiently nervous about lending this much money that I borrowed his camera as security. Within less than a week he repaid the money and reclaimed his camera. I had no idea, then, that repayment in under a week was something of a record for him. Anyway, although David never did go on the proposed parachuting course, I became increasingly involved in the Dangerous Sports Club and its bizarre activities.

My chance to do a bungee jump soon arrived. Previously, the only platforms used for bungee jumping were bridges, such as Clifton, the Golden Gate, and the Royal Gorge, and the hot-air balloon. The Club had made money out of this by selling the event to newspapers and TV companies, which was successful when bungee jumping still had novelty value, but obviously would lose its appeal with repetition. To test the market for live display bungee jumps, David had offered to present a bungee performance at an outdoor, summer show. The organisers would pay a fee for this, naturally smaller than the fees paid by television, but enough to make it worth while. The jumps would be made from a mobile, telescopic crane about 170ft high.

The night before the show I met Dave Turnbull and we left Oxford together for the village of Braishfield, near Southampton. We stayed that night in a bed and breakfast called the Wessex Guest House. The next morning we arrived at the show ground, and set about attaching the bungee ropes to the crane's telescopic boom. Jumpers would be carried up and down in a little cage suspended from the main lifting cable of the crane. When we got about two thirds of the way up, we could catch the free end of the bungee rope and continue up to the top, where we would attach the bungee cord to the jumper's harness. When the jump was made and the bouncing died down, we could lower the cage to the level of the jumper, who would then climb back in.

This system seemed to work well enough, and the audience enjoyed the display. It was a hot, sunny afternoon and the show was going well. Soon it was my turn to jump. I had been up and down a few times to help other people jump, and found that I was nervous of being in the cage because the crane's lifting cable looked so thin and flimsy. I felt more secure once I was connected to the thick, strong bungee ropes, but was still not entirely at ease.

Between 100ft and 200ft there seems to be a height of maximum anxiety. It is high enough to kill you if you fall, yet low enough to see every detail on the ground and talk to people below. If you go higher, perhaps in an aircraft, the ground begins to resemble a map, and the sensation of height is less intimidating. Most bungee jumps are made from 100-200ft heights, and so can require more nerve than a parachute jump from 2,000ft or higher. I was certainly anxious while awaiting my jump. As it turned out, I had every right to be.

I was wearing a full-body climbing harness. It had a tangle of straps and buckles which all met somehow at the middle of the chest, where there was an attachment point. I was attached to the free end of the bungee rope using two karabiners (mountaineers' clips which have a wide range of uses) and two or three loops of knotted climbing rope. Once attached to the bungee rope, and at the top of the crane, I was ready to jump. Someone held the loose bungee rope to one side, out of my way. I climbed over the side of the cage, but remained clinging on to the outside. Little gusts of wind would swing the cage around to face different directions, and I was not quite sure which was the best way to face. I dithered, but nobody became irritated or made sarcastic remarks. Looking down, I could see blades of grass rippling in the breeze a long way below. I summoned my nerve and let go.

The bungee rope was about 60ft long. I fell freely to this point, which took two seconds, although it felt longer at the time. As I let go of the cage, I had that stomach-left-behind feeling you get in a lift, and began to accelerate towards the grass. Jumping from aeroplanes was nothing like this, and I waited tensely for the rope to stop my fall. I was still looking down, and in fact I was falling in the normal position of a skydiver, belly to earth, which turned out to be my undoing – this was not my lucky day.

I had expected to feel some relief when the bungee rope tightened and slowed me down, but what I actually felt was a sudden impact in my face. Although I was momentarily dazed by the blow, I immediately realised I could not see out of my right eye. Fast as the pain rose, fear rose faster, as a worried crane driver lowered me to the ground.

Looking back on it later, I found I could remember the sensation of bouncing up and down, and I could even enjoy it in retrospect, but at the time I could only think of whether I would be blinded permanently. I could ignore the pain, but the suspense was killing me. How bad was the injury? Would it get better? With one hand, I explored my face and could feel the eyeball. Well, at least it had not burst. There was hope yet. I realised that when I had reached the natural length of the bungee rope, moving at over fifty-feet-per-second, it had suddenly tightened, and the knotted climbing rope had slammed into my face. Probably a knot had hit me square on the eyeball. For once, the Club's traditional beginners' luck had deserted us.

As at most of these sort of outdoor events, the St John Ambulance Association were providing medical cover. They put me in their ambulance and tried to comfort me on the way to hospital. At first I found this a bit trying, as they couldn't tell how serious my injury was, and until I knew that, I could hardly lie back and relax. However I was very grateful to them for being there, and my mood improved a bit when I began to be able to see light once again with my right eye.

By the time a doctor examined me, I was suffering from shock and throwing up, but recovering more sight. I was bandaged up, which may have been good for me, but was frustrating because I could not tell how much sight I was getting back. I was kept in overnight. The next day I was still a bit of a mess, but felt I ought to tell my parents anyway. They were naturally horrified, and made plans to visit. They could not arrive in time to visit that day, so stayed the night, by one of those quirks which often accompanied Club activities, at the Wessex Guest House.

When I was able to take the bandage off, I found I was recovering most of my vision, but not the patch right in the middle. Today, the injured eye is still able to see, but slightly distorted, leading to a curious double-vision effect. Near the centre is a permanent blind spot. Also, my pupil remains permanently dilated, which often gets an inquisitive response from other people. Some have even found it attractive, a small consolation for the loss of good vision. Today, although I can just read a newspaper with the right eye, it is the left eye that does the real work.

*

Most of my family thought I had been very stupid to do the jump, and I could hardly tell them that I was actually quite keen to do it again, as soon as possible. I realised that what had happened was preventable, and that bungee jumping could, in fact, be done very safely. However, part of the problem was the fact that it wasn't a 'proper' sport and was carried on by the Dangerous Sports Club, unlike skydiving, which was responsibly organised and so did not worry my folks so much. In the end, I followed a policy of just not telling them very much about what I was doing. It was easier than trying to explain.

6.

Across the Alps by Pink Elephant

'If in doubt, think Fellini.'
– David Kirke

In these drab, grey days, nobody finds themselves playing a grand piano at the top of a very steep ski slope, accelerating downhill, and being overtaken by a man in a bathtub and a couple eating dinner off antique furniture, with a string quartet playing Mozart in the background. At least, not without the help of psychedelic substances. In the early-Eighties, though, we had a better way: the Dangerous Sports Club surreal ski race.

As far as I could tell (it was later disputed), the idea for the ski race arose during a bonfire night party in November 1982. My contemporary at Oxford and skydiving friend, Henry Robinson, and Hugo Spowers, who had graduated in engineering that summer, bought 200-feet of washing line and used it to experiment with parascending, towing Henry's parachute behind a Land Rover. Henry, whose athletic frame and good looks were rewarded by female attention which he blithely accepted as of right and mostly ignored, was a regular partner of mine in RW skydiving and a fellow physics student. Hugo was a motor racing devotee who wore a flourishing moustache which lent him a dashing, rakish appearance. Both were aware that washing line is not strong enough for aviation purposes, but then, flying with dodgy equipment was routine in the Club.

Although the line kept breaking, they were able to tow each other high enough into the air to provide a worthwhile afternoon's amusement for the Guy Fawkes night party gathered at Wittenham Clumps, just south of Oxford. Around the fire that evening, Hugo and Philip Oppenheim began to speculate on the possibility of staging a bicycle race down the Matterhorn. Philip had been one of the first Oxford students to get involved in the Club, although he left it later to go into politics, and he became a Conservative MP and junior trade minister.

In getting a bicycle down the Matterhorn, any route or technique would be permitted, the winner being the person who got from top to bottom in the least time. Clearly, you could use a parachute to glide down the steeper parts, and you could either carry or ride the bicycle the rest of the way down. The idea seemed so good that it began to take shape as a project for the coming winter sports season. Over the following days they talked about it more, and the idea developed. Why limit it to bicycles, when more interesting modes of transport could be just as amusing? The object of the race changed from simple top to bottom speed, to creating the most surreal method which could be used as a substitute for the more conventional ways of getting down a mountain. Finally, even the Matterhorn was dropped from the event, as St Moritz seemed far more suitable now that the idea was to poke fun at ordinary winter sports by devising a new one.

Hugo, who was going skiing around Christmas, took a train to St Moritz to investigate holding the race there. He went to the tourist office and spoke to one Dr Danuser, who liked the plan and agreed without quibble to host the event. Hugo came back and set about organising it. He already had several ideas in mind for different approaches to the challenge, and kept coming up with more. He went to see Elton John playing at the Hammersmith Odeon one night, and spent the whole concert wondering how to mount a grand piano on skis. (His solution involved building two fixed skids on the back legs of the piano, and a steerable one on the front leg, a combination which turned out to work very well.)

David Kirke set out to find a sponsor for the event. David was gaining the confidence needed to ask companies to risk their reputations on ridiculous events, and although it was a long search, he succeeded in finding a company looking for offbeat publicity. He managed to persuade the makers of Long Life beer to open their corporate wallet, and for only £5000 they got tremendous coverage, the ski race lending itself very well to brand name display. This also began a long tradition of Club sponsorship by brewers and distillers, which happened so often that it was obviously no accident.

Most of the devices were constructed by Hugo, who was working for a racing car constructor and had access to workshop facilities. Working at night, together with Chris Baker (who had just returned from the USA), he built a range of ski machines the like of which had never been seen before. The devices included wheelchairs, a bathtub, a punt, a stepladder, an ironing board, a lavatory, a tandem bicycle, a settee, and magnums of champagne, all ingeniously mounted on skis. Further up the scale of grandeur there was a vintage electric invalid carriage, a Louis XIV dining suite, a grand piano, and a rowing boat mounted on skis. The boat was a long, narrow, racing-eight like those used in the University Boat Race. All of this took a great deal of work to create. Hugo felt later that he was not duly credited for his efforts. Whether this complaint was justified or not, it was to grow into a bitter argument which nearly put an end to the ski race at its outset.

In his own words: *Xan Rufus-Isaacs*

I have a vivid memory of Hugo having this huge workshop up at Shepherd's Bush. Hugo was obviously doing 99.9% of the work, and was complaining about others turning up drunk and getting in the way and not helping at all, but isn't that always the story? And then on the film they made of it, there's Dave saying 'Yes, Hugo and I stayed up until three in the morning trying to get these machines to work,' and I certainly remember what Hugo had to say about that particular comment. But you know, Dodge [David] was very much the inspiration behind this, he managed to get the Swiss to agree to have it, and in his somewhat chaotic way, he pulled the whole thing together.

St Moritz has always been a very up-market ski resort, catering to the wealthy and fashionable. The Cresta Run is located there, built by the English in 1885, but its appeal today rests more on snobbery than daring. The upper class image of St Moritz attracted the social dinosaurs of the British press, who were delighted to cover such a photogenic event, and incidentally to visit a posh ski resort on expenses. The Club duly gathered in the Park Hotel, in St Moritz, in early March. A film crew was there to record the event. In the same spirit as the Club members, the film crew were not being paid, but had come along to have fun and to make a low-budget production. It says a lot for the fun atmosphere in the Club, its reputation, the appeal of the ski race as an idea, and David's ability to charm them, that such busy people would give up their time, even in return for a free ski trip.

The day of the race was snowy and visibility was poor. Not put off by bad weather, Club members rode up the Corviglia inclined railway, and assembled their devices in a shed at the top of the piste, to the musical accompaniment of the *Not* The Amadeus String Quartet, who had been invited along to provide a suitable atmosphere.

The 'race' was not a timed contest in the conventional sense, grace and style being more important than simple speed. Ski devices were launched downhill one by one, starting with smaller ones like the wheelchairs and lavatories, and working up to the more absurd and unstable.

Some machines went faster than others, with the vintage electric invalid carriage among the fastest. When it finally overturned, Mike Boyd-Maunsell, the driver, was thrown out, flying some way from the carriage. He got up and hobbled back up the slope, past his wreckage, complaining of a strained back. The rowing-eight were less fortunate, failing to reach such exciting speed. Because it had no effective steering, the forty-foot long boat steadily turned to the left until, broadside on to the slope and standing on legs three feet high, it rolled over. The crew was poured out and oars cascaded in all directions, while the splintered boat came to rest like a dead insect, with its twisted ski-legs waving in the air.

It was being filmed at the time by Roger Wood, the regular Club photographer, who took what I consider to be one of the finest pieces of Dangerous Sports Club film ever made. As the boat turned over and people and oars went flying in all directions, Roger spotted a bottle falling out of the boat which began to roll down the hill. He kept filming for another thirty seconds, a good decision by a cameraman with very limited supplies of film, and slowly the bottle rolled and spun down the hill, leaving the chaos of the boat crash behind, finally coming to a halt just in front of the camera, with the label clearly visible: 'J&B Rare', a brand of Scotch whisky which at the time, was advertised by the slogan 'It can be found…' It summed up the event completely.

The piano fared rather better. Played by Hubie Gibbs, who was a brilliant classical pianist, and Hugo, who was drunk, it navigated the course right to the bottom. The image of the piano was very popular with the press and was featured in several newspapers the next day. It was, in my view, the highlight of the day's 'Avant-Skiing' (as we called it).

Despite the weather, the race was enjoyed by everybody (except David Kirke, who was in hospital at the time, having broken his leg on a bungee jump), and naturally demanded celebration. The Club were, for the most part, staying in the Park Hotel in St Moritz-Bad. The film crew wanted to round off their footage with some shots of the ensuing apres-ski party, and encouraged everyone to play up for the camera. They didn't take much encouraging. A chair-vaulting contest began, followed by a diving competition involving a large bucket of water filled with ice and beer cans. The hotel staff were looking increasingly nervous, and their worst fears were soon justified.

In his own words: *Mike Fitzroy*

The first ski race was also my first Club activity. I was in the Guards and had been posted at St James' Palace, and one evening there things got a bit out of hand and I swung from one of the chandeliers, like Errol Flynn, only it broke and fell right on top of me. Fortunately there wasn't much damage, we just hung it up again, but I got into deep shit over it. Anyway, in St Moritz, I was talking to Hugo and suggested he should try it. He took me seriously and of course, exactly the same thing happened, only this time the chandelier was completely smashed.

The chandelier broke with a noise Hugo would never forget (he was, after all, underneath it at the time). The sound of smashed glass fragments cascading around the floor was one of those expensive noises, like the sound of a crashing Rolls-Royce, or a shattering Ming vase, which has an immediate sobering effect. Instantly, the high-spirited crowd sensed that things may have gone a bit too far. The film director was delighted, realising that it would provide an ideal end for his film and improve his chances of selling it to American cable TV.

In his own words: *Xan Rufus-Isaacs*

It was at the party after the race, at the Park Hotel, that the chandelier incident took place. There was a string quartet playing and someone discovered that if you hurled a can of Long Life beer the length of this ballroom and it hit the wall at the other end, it would explode, and if it hit a light fitting, it would take out the light fitting in a pretty spectacular fashion. Soon there were cans of beer being flung hard from one end of the room to the other. Fitz [Mike Fitzroy] was climbing around, jumping over tables. Then it ended up with Hugo on Tim Hunt's shoulders, trying to get on to the chandelier, which of course he managed to do. Just as Tim lets him go and he's swinging there, the management of the hotel come in and we heard this terrible 'Nein! Nein! Nein!' and the whole chandelier came down.

Everybody realised it had gone way over the top and it was time to get out otherwise there would be unpleasant repercussions. There were forty or fifty people trying to get out, and the Swiss ahead of us running up and locking all the doors and barring all the exits because they wanted to keep us in there. Everyone went up the main stairs, and at the top, on the mezzanine floor, there were these big windows, and people were jumping out not really knowing what was underneath. In fact there was a huge snowdrift. You ended up jumping on top of somebody who had just jumped out, and you knew there were going to be about twenty people jumping out in the next few seconds, and they are all going to land on you. Anyway, apart from Hugo who was pretty well cut up, everyone got out all right.

I took Hugo to the clinic to get sewn up…

The value of the chandelier was put at 10,000 Francs, about £3000. Hugo didn't have the money, and his passport was impounded by the Swiss police. Nobody was quite sure how the bill would be met. There was a lot of sympathy for Hugo, who had done so much to make the ski race happen and to give everyone such fun. A whip round was organised, and raised about £500, enough for Hugo to be allowed home. Some felt the film crew, having encouraged such behaviour to begin with, should take some responsibility. Some thought that the Club should contribute out of the sponsorship money and any income from sale of the film.

The Club left St Moritz with most of the damage still to be paid for, and bitter recriminations began. The Swiss became increasingly angry and made it clear that no more Club events would be permitted until the bill was met.

This was a situation the Club had not faced before. Not that there had never been collateral damage, but the cost had always been within the pocket of those who caused it, and considered an occupational hazard. Such an expensive breakage was a different matter. The bottom line was that Hugo had to pay for the breakage, but other considerations were involved. The most important was the ownership of the event itself. Despite the fact that David had arranged the sponsorship, Hugo was not happy with David's way of running things, and was determined to organise his own sport in future, without David's involvement. He realised that with a professional approach and some cost control discipline, the whole field of adventure sports could be a good one in which to work. In particular, Hugo wanted to organise the next ski race himself. David, on the other hand, felt that his company, Dangerous Sports Club Ltd, owned the ski race, and was equally determined to establish control of it.

In the end, Hugo raised the money and paid the bill just in time for the next ski race to go ahead, but the real damage was to the Club itself. Hugo and David were in a full-blown feud, and Hugo began to organise the next ski race on his own, under the marginally different name of the Alternative Sports Club. He soon realised that sponsors were unwilling to back an event whose ownership was in dispute. It began to look as if there would be no ski race.

In the end, Hugo felt it was all more trouble than he cared to face, and David organised a ski race in 1984 under the name of the Dangerous Sports Club. For some years afterwards, David and Hugo refused to speak to each other, though they are on better terms again now.

Once the bill was paid, the Swiss were comparatively happy, although we were not welcome at the Park Hotel again. The second ski race took place in 1984, without overall sponsorship, members paying their own costs. This time around, we got bigger ideas. The potential of the event was unlimited – or so we thought. All we needed were more elaborate and artistic devices. The old bathtub and wheelchair machines were used again, since they were available and were fun to ride. Several new devices were added, raising the level of humour and spectacle.

Tommy Leigh-Pemberton commissioned an inflatable pink elephant from a manufacturer of, well, inflatable pink elephants. Tommy was, perhaps, the Club member who best fitted our press stereotype. He had been to Eton before studying at Oxford, and was a boisterous younger son of an upper class banker. People like him were often called Hooray Henries, and generally spoken of and written about with derision. The English press has an absurd obsession with class, which distorts the way they view our society; in the Club, we accepted that nobody chooses their parents, and anyway, there is no room for social snobbery in the Real

World. In fact, Tommy was very down to earth, unpretentious, unselfish and kind, as well as being tremendous fun to have around. The elephant, or Nellie, as it was rather unimaginatively called, was really more orange than pink in colour and was mounted on four toboggans. She had an oddly serious look, almost stern, unlike Tommy, who considered himself naked without a cheerful expression.

The replica Louis Quinze dining table and two chairs, veterans of the first race, were remounted on a metal frame constructed for the purpose. There was room for two diners, two waiters and one person at the back to steer the front ski using pedal-operated push-rods. It was a sophisticated mechanism, and very effective. One technical point we had learned the first time round was that it was quite pointless to fit brakes. Most people who tried to make some sort of control mechanism for a surrealist skiing device the first year, had fitted brakes. Sadly, we found, all brakes do is slow you down. Most machines were too slow anyway. What is much more important is a steering mechanism. The ability to stay on the groomed piste is all-important. If you stay on, you keep going, unless your machine breaks up or falls over. If you go off the piste, you run into either spectators or soft snow, both of which will slow you down and ultimately stop you.

For the second race, I built a roller-disco, complete with a dance floor, and a ball covered in little mirrors hanging over it. The disco equipment came from a sound equipment hire shop in Oxford, but was not, sadly, in working order, saving me the very tricky decision of what records to play on the way down the slope. At one stage I borrowed a ghetto-blaster to put inside the disco unit, and started to worry about what music to play; then its owner discovered what I was planning to do, took it back, and saved me losing any more sleep. The dance floor was made from sheets of plywood, with skis nailed underneath. The skis were ex-rental. In fact, I obtained all the materials free. I had learnt how to persuade people to give things away for nothing, a technique which underpinned a good deal of what the Club did over the years.

In order to share travel costs, I drove to St Moritz with Roger Wood, his girlfriend, and Nellie, in my aged Ford Cortina. I used to get some sarcastic remarks about that car, which was hardly stylish, but it was relatively cheap and it got me around. Carrying three people and an elephant, though, it only just made it over the high Alpine passes.

We stayed at the Hotel Chanterella this time, which was an old building perched half way up a mountain, presumably considered to be sufficiently far from the people who had been offended the first time round. In fact it was nearer to the slope used for the race, and conveniently close to the inclined railway. Getting all the machines into the railway carriages was not easy, even though they were in pieces. A few of the larger items had to be towed up behind piste-rolling tractors.

The slope, a 'black run', was intimidatingly steep, at least to a novice avant-skier such as me. I think those with some normal skiing experience realised it was perfect for the devices we had built. Those which didn't fall apart would reach a terrific speed. Those which did fall apart usually made an acceptably entertaining wipe-out in the snow. Snow is very forgiving, and generally even the fastest wipe-outs ended with the riders getting up laughing. Hubie Gibbs was the only serious casualty. He was riding a racing car body shell, which rolled at high speed, leaving him concussed. David Kirke was similarly, but less seriously, hurt when his Sinclair C5 rolled. It was becoming clear that devices which were liable to roll, particularly if they enclosed the rider, could be a problem.

My disco didn't get up as much speed as I had hoped, and about two thirds of the way down it ran off-piste and ground to a halt. It didn't roll over or break up, in fact it was nothing much to laugh at – it would have been better if I had carried the roller-skating passengers I had hoped for, and played loud disco music. As a sculptural comment on the social life of a ski resort, I don't believe it managed to say much. Still, I was new to this form of artistic expression. I would learn in time. Soon after this, I got a more exciting ride in another machine.

We had obtained a full size model horse from the National Theatre props department. Carefully modelled, and with a saddle and reins, it would not have been out of place in the charge of the Light Brigade. It was mounted on skis, was steerable, and was ridden by Cosmo Hulton, Ed's younger brother. Cosmo was short, with the expression of an innocent abroad, which sometimes led people to underestimate him. He had the rotund physique of a true Sultan among sofa spuds, which reinforced the effect. He had already put in a very fine performance on an exercise cycle, which reached a magnificent speed before falling over in a huge spray of snow. Cosmo was finely dressed in hunting pink, as was David Kirke, who rode beneath the horse, operating the steering gear. However, the one-horse St Moritz hunt could not proceed without a quarry, which is where I came in.

Scenery constructor Steve Smithwick had built a hedge on a three-ski undercarriage, the front one being steerable, and this was the fox's cover. The hedge could carry two, so Steve sat on the back. I dressed in a furry suit, not instantly recognisable as a fox, but good enough for Cosmo to give a Tally-Ho. I was steering the front ski using pedals.

We set off, just in front of the horse, and quickly gathered speed. The hedge was fast and steered well. The horse was also making good speed. It seemed we had a real race on our hands. Suddenly, the mounting of my front ski failed, and the hedge instantly disintegrated in a cloud of snow, earth and greenery. Steve and I got up, with only small bruises, and the first thing we saw was a very heavy, very fast-moving horse about to run us down. It wasn't going to stop and it didn't want a lump of sugar. We leaped to one side as the horse smashed through the wreckage of the hedge. It was charging down the slope like Red Rum on the last furlong, and David was steering it with gusto. They almost made it to the bottom, but hit a mogul and went over on one side. Cosmo was thrown clear, while the horse's head broke off and was flung down the hill. David was winded. Steve and I looked down the hill; after the day's sport, the piste was dotted with small pieces of strange debris. David picked up the horse's head and began the slow climb back up.

*

The second ski race was tremendous sport for us, and was also appreciated by a wider audience. It was given a full two minutes on the main TV news bulletin that evening – not bad considering it took place on budget day, when light-hearted items don't usually get a look in. Jill Morrell, the Sports Editor of the TV news company UPITN who had covered the race, wrote to say that the item they transmitted had been very popular, reaching a world audience of 900 million people. This was the biggest audience ever known for a winter sports event, Olympics included, which struck me as meaningful in some way. In the Sixties, The Beatles were bigger than Jesus. In the Seventies, Abba were bigger than Volvo. But in the Eighties, we had (for two minutes, at least) been bigger than the Olympics! Was there a cultural message in this? Most television serves only to define normal behaviour, so could we claim to be striking a blow for the individual and for the imagination by using TV to display some lateral thinking, and beating the ratings of the more predictable sports? Perhaps so; but later, I got the impression that most people thought we were just another group of camera hounds who enjoyed attention. Whichever way you look at it, at least our kind of sport was a good laugh, and nobody took steroids.

If nothing else, we had obviously found something that, like bungee jumping, was firmly identifiable with the Dangerous Sports Club, and made first-rate TV entertainment. If only we could make it pay! Looking back, the ski races were the most popular and enjoyable Club events. They attracted the highest number of participants of any Club activity, and had consistently astronomical TV audience figures. They were fun, had novelty value, and were enjoyed by those involved, by the press, and by the audience. They were among the most widely appreciated performance art events of the Eighties, although run on a shoestring. They were, in short, about the nearest we came to success, in our own terms. They didn't make us money. Still, you can't have everything, and we had what mattered.

7.

Bad Taste can be Habit-Forming

'The path of excess leads to the
tower of wisdom.'
– William Blake

Around the time of the first ski race, the concept of bungee jumping had spread to the point where almost everybody had heard about it, but almost no-one had actually seen it. There was a lot of public interest, and this meant that we were able to find well-paid display work. Most displays involved jumping from mobile cranes as we had done at Braishfield, but there were occasional exceptions. Once, we were asked to open a travel agency in Oxford High Street. Hugo Spowers, Dave Turnbull and I set up a ladder projecting out, rather shakily, from the top of the building, which was just three floors high, and we dangled a short bungee rope from it. David Kirke, who had arranged the job, left us to it; as usual, he preferred to delegate any task involving calculation, knotting, welding, fastening, load-bearing, or technical matters of any kind, to people with degrees in engineering – not that this guaranteed competent work, of course.

Although this flimsy ladder arrangement allowed only a modest sort of jump, the crowd in the High Street below us found it entertaining, perhaps because of the double-decker buses passing below us, which were an additional hazard not commonly found in bungee jumping. After this display, we returned to more conventional jumping from cranes at outdoor shows.

Bungee jumping was not the only commercial activity going on. David had rented an office in Foley Street, Soho, at the heart of London's film and independent TV industry. Following the cinema release of *The History of the Dangerous Sports Club*, he was hoping to receive offers of further work in medium- (or large-) budget film productions. But his contacts in the area only led to small-time work. One weekend, a group of us acted in a TV commercial for a Sunday newspaper which was running a story about the rescue of some hostages from Iran. The commercial was to be made to a tight schedule and with a tight budget, which certainly did not stretch to hiring twelve Equity-registered stunt-men at Equity rates, so we stood in.

The location was a derelict part of Battersea power station. The set decorators painted one wall with a giant mural of Ayatollah Khomeini, and positioned a number of fireworks around the set. Our job was to climb out of windows, abseil down ropes, and run across the site while the fireworks were going off. This was intended to re-create the escape of some American hostages held by the Khomeini regime. It was great fun for me, as a young student, to be involved in a TV production. In between setting up the abseiling and testing fireworks, I chatted up the production assistant and got invited to the cameraman's party. The other Club members involved enjoyed it too; but while it made us a modest amount of money, it was hardly the sort of thing for which the Club could claim worldwide renown.

Nor did we get any more such TV work, as Equity heard about it and fined the production company for using non-union actors. Such bullying by Equity was, of course, done out of pure self-interest, although the official Equity line is that they do it to protect people like me. (I have always felt worried when people try to protect me, especially from myself). The Club often came up against protectionism, as for example when trying to establish a bank to be called 'Schwindler und Vraud' to provide certain inno-vative and amusing financial services. This was an idea David had wanted to follow up for years, ever since he and Ed Hulton had agreed that the existing banks were too pompous and irritating for their tastes. It would at least have amused David to be able to pay parking tickets with a cheque drawn on Schwindler und Vraud, but it turns out that you are not allowed simply to start a bank, the way you can start any other business. The declared reason for such laws is to protect depositors, although people willing to entrust their money to a bank called Schwindler und Vraud are probably well beyond protection. The banking regulation system, which happily tolerated BCCI for so long, would not allow a comedy or surrealist bank.

Eventually it became clear that there was insufficient work offered, or even in prospect, to pay for the office in Foley Street, and it was closed in 1983. This was a sort of high-tide mark in the business affairs of the Club. From the early days the Club had grown fast, and the projects had become bigger and better; but now we had reached a point at which we could no longer expand. There were other problems as well.

I may have suffered the first permanent injury from bungee jumping, but I was not the last to get hurt. David Kirke broke his leg doing a bungee jump from a crane in Preston in 1983, just before the first ski race, and he nearly suffered an even worse fate when experimenting with catapult bungee jumps. In catapult jumps, the jumper is tied down to the ground while the bungee is stretched, then the jumper is released and flies upwards. If you put enough tension in the bungee rope, you can get real, bone-crushing acceleration on release. The jumper can even fly clear over the top of the crane, which is not possible in a 'normal' jump. Catapults are sometimes offered today as a soft option for those who haven't the nerve to jump off the top, but the way we did them they were definitely not for wimps. The first time David tried it, he thought it would add to the spectacle if the release was accomplished by blasting through the rope which held him down, using a shotgun. To do this, it was necessary to fire the gun at the rope between David's legs, where it was attached to a block of concrete. Unfortunately for him, some rebounding shotgun pellets caught him in the foot; he was lucky it wasn't somewhere more painful. After that we stuck to the more mundane method of cutting the rope with a knife (although I was once cut loose by a flamboyantly-wielded Samurai sword).

A much worse accident happened in July 1983 during a crane jumping show at the village of Potterspury. Members of the Club, finding that bungee jumping from a crane quickly becomes routine, decided to try adjusting the length of the rope until they could just touch the ground at the bottom of the bounce. This is an obvious extension of bungee jumping which is commonly practiced today, usually by splashing down into water. However, in those days it was not a well known trick, and Hugo Spowers, one of the experimenters, got into big trouble by making his rope too long.

Like several members of the Club, Hugo could be opinionated and preferred to try his own ideas before listening to advice. So, when his first jump did not come close enough to the ground, he decided to add more rope to the line so that he could touch the grass; but, although a couple of others suggested smaller increases in rope length, he extended his rope by a full fifteen feet more than he had used on the previous attempt, jumped out, and smashed into the grass below sickeningly hard.

Fortunately, at this time almost all bungee jumps were made in the upright position. Ankle harnesses are more popular today, allowing a head-first dive, but in those days we preferred to be upright. If he had gone head first, Hugo would certainly have been killed. As it was, he broke both legs and his pelvis. Following the chandelier incident and the argument over the ski race, Hugo already had a very strained relationship with David. The injury he suffered, although his own fault, put him off further involvement in the Club for several years. There is a happy ending to this story; he now holds a particularly good party around the anniversary of his accident, to celebrate still being alive.

Through bungee jumping accidents, Hugo and David had both came close to ending up in wheelchairs. In fact the Club logo was a wheelchair, and it was emblazoned on a bow tie which had been produced in small numbers. David used to say that, before a Club 'Awayday', he used to notice people in wheelchairs far more often than usual, which was termed Coincidental Wheelchair Sighting, or CWS for short. A CWS was to be regarded as a positive omen. This morbid sort of humour, which is typical of people who go in for dangerous sports of all kinds, was sometimes considered to be in bad taste, but only by the able-bodied; we never met a chairbound person who found it at all offensive. Several chairbound people made bungee jumps and loved it; and it is a real joy to see the reaction of a blind person to the experience. All the same, the use of the wheelchair logo was perhaps a little brash and provocative. It invited the disapproval of those we would now describe as politically correct, just as the sedan chair joke at Kilimanjaro courted misunderstanding, and provoked an argument with Julian Grant. There was no malice in either case, but no great sensitivity either.

Bad taste can become habit forming. Before deciding to run the Club as a full-time occupation, David had worked in publishing and journalism, and he still wrote on a freelance basis. In early 1984, he wrote an article about the Club for a magazine called *Men Only*, part of Paul Raymond's soft-porn publishing group. The article, predictably entitled Cunning Stunts, needed pictures, and a date was set for a photo shoot. The article described bungee jumping from Clifton suspension bridge, but rather than go to Bristol, we were asked to meet on Albert Bridge in west London. About half a dozen Club members turned out, along with a few simple props such as a wheelchair, some bungee rope and a bottle of champagne. Nevile Player, editor of *Men Only*, came with his photographer and a nude model. (In *Men Only*, even an article about sport has to have pictures of scantily-clad dolly birds.) While none of us objected too strongly to this, it was quite early in the morning (in order to avoid heavy traffic) and not particularly warm. The poor girl had to run around in her underwear trying to look attractive despite the cold, while the rest of us posed fully dressed.

Nevile Player was a genial man who was sufficiently intrigued by the first article to commission several more from David. For some years, David contributed a monthly piece for *Men Only* under the pen name Mad Jack (after the eighteenth-century eccentric Jack Lytton). Nevile did not quite fit the dirty-raincoat image of a man who spends a considerable part of his working life selecting shapely young women from model agencies, and paying them to take off all their clothes. I suppose anything can become routine after a while. Nevile did not become a member of the Club, but we saw him from time to time, at social events and the like. The articles David wrote were fairly short, and the monthly fee was not very much. The main advantage for David was that he was officially a Gentleman of the Press, and therefore entitled to a vast range of freebies. Writing mostly about food, drink and travel, he was able to score free samples in all three categories, which he good-naturedly shared with others. Whoever coined the expression 'There's no such thing as a free lunch,' obviously wasn't a journalist.

Perhaps the best freebie which he shared with me was a tour of Scottish distilleries. Air tickets to Scotland, accommodation, and the distillery tour were all provided by the Distillers company, owners of such brands as Johnny Walker. David's girlfriend was unable to go, so I was offered the spare ticket. We were entertained at the Cardhu distillery by the manager, and offered generous free samples of his product, an offer we accepted gratefully. He also offered us a cassette tape of himself singing traditional Scottish songs, an offer we accepted politely.

We were able to obtain all kinds of goods on loan from manu-facturers. On rare occasions, these were even returned. We garnered some useful office equipment in this fashion, including an early kind of word processor which I used for producing the frequent but irregular *Nurdorandum*, or Club newsletter, which was circulated to members. David always gained particular satis-faction from getting something for nothing, to the extent that if ever left unsupervised near someone else's telephone, he would make as many long-distance calls as he could, just to say hello to people he knew, a habit he called 'internationalling'. This expres-sion was part of the peculiar language I termed Kirkespeak. At its best, Kirkespeak could be very entertaining and was widely imitated in the Club. At its worst, it was impossible to understand. I got used to interpreting David's own terminology, and to his frequent use of anecdotes and quotes as a substitute for reasoned argument, but I could see it confused people not accustomed to it.

*

The connection with Nevile Player led to another curious diver-sion, in April 1984, when *Men Only* was preparing an article about off-road motorcycles and three– or four-wheel 'bikes', which were becoming popular at the time. To get some pictures of them being ridden, he suggested that some of us should go to Weston-Super-Mare for a weekend. While we played with these toys, he could get his pictures. We duly rode them along the beach, which is used by local youths as a sort of racetrack. At one point we were asked to stand around in an area of the dunes, keeping a lookout for the easily offended, while Nevile and his photographer took naughty pictures of girls draping themselves over the motorcycles. The photographer did his job well, and the pictures made it look as though the girls were in the Bahamas, but in fact they were absolutely brass-monkey freezing and again I felt very sorry for them. There was one in particular I sympathised with, who told me she really wanted to be a serious Shakespearean actress, and was only doing nude modelling and striptease work to get an Equity card – another victim of restrictive practices. I sometimes wonder whether she ever got to play Ophelia.

After all this hard work, we retired to a hotel for a little light refreshment, while the photographer and the models carried on with their work in the hotel swimming pool. We were supposed to do a few more motorcycle pictures the next day, but as it turned out, I was not able to take part. Waking early, I decided to try the hotel hot tub, as I had not used one before. When I got out of it, I dived straight into the swimming pool to cool off. Unfortunately the pool was not as deep as I thought, and I hit my head very hard on the bottom. A large and extremely colourful bruise came up, which quite put me off my breakfast. It faded over a few days, but this episode completely cured me of the desire to dive head-first into water, which I have since been told is a leading cause of neck-down paralysis.

It also made me think. If I had been knocked out in the pool, nobody was around to pull me out. I had come fairly close to being either drowned or paralysed in a completely ridiculous situation, surrounded by a hotel full of nude models and lecherous free-loaders. Taking a risk for the sake of an adventure was one thing, but making on-the-cheap TV commercials or appearing in top-shelf magazines was something else, and this wasn't what I had become involved for.

It was time for something bigger and better, and both David and I were working on projects which would make that summer a memorable one – but separately.

8.

The Last Volcano

'The biggest danger in life is not taking
adventures.'
– George Mallory

Hang-gliding was always David Kirke's favourite form of
flight. In the summer of 1984, he planned an expedition to
Ecuador, with the aim of hang-gliding from the volcanoes
Chimbarazo and Cotopaxi. This ambitious enterprise took a long
time to arrange, and he put a lot of effort into obtaining free mountaineering clothing and equipment. He was not able, though, to
find an overall sponsor who would meet the considerable cost of
the trip.

I was invited to join the expedition. I was not put off by my total
lack of hang-gliding experience, but I had other reservations. At
the time I was a research student in Oxford, working for a PhD. It
was perfectly all right for me to take time off if I wanted to; after
all, if my research fell behind because I spent too much time on
other pursuits, I was the one who would suffer. Even so, I felt that
two whole months was too long to be away from the lab. David
scoffed at this excuse, and he was right in a sense; if I had been
determined to go, I would have left my research to take care of
itself.

An even more persuasive reason to stay at home was the cost. I
was an organiser of the Club and I regularly worked on the less
glamorous, money-spinning jobs we did, such as bungee jumping
displays at outdoor shows. In return, when we had sponsorship
for a good Awayday, my costs might be partly paid out of the
income from the sponsor. Even then, I was often financially
embarrassed when we got to the bar in the evening and I couldn't

keep up with those who had deeper pockets. (The Club attracted many young, single men without families or mortgages, who had healthy disposable incomes.) The trip to Ecuador, though, was not sponsored, and each participant had to pay their own way. Mountaineering trips to South America were way out of my reach. David also scoffed at this reason, as his attitude was always to ignore the limits of his purse, and follow his dreams come what may. There is something to be said for that attitude – up to a point – but I was not yet ready to follow that path.

David, seeing through my excuses, realised that I doubted that the venture would succeed. For one thing, I did not believe that enough members of the expedition were able to make it to the top of the mountain. The climbing involved would be very demanding, much more so than Kilimanjaro, but there were some people in the group who could barely carry a hang-glider at sea level, and had no determination or commitment. They were, essentially, going for a holiday.

David did not appreciate being told this, and to flatter me, he pointed out that if I committed myself to the project, it would improve the chances of it succeeding. But feeling underconfident in both myself and the expedition, I chose to stay behind.

Others were less faint-hearted; Wally Blacker, Mike Fitzroy, Cosmo Hulton (Ed's younger brother) and Roger Wood were all going. In all, David assembled a crew of fourteen people, mostly fliers, but including three film crew and a couple of non-flying members. The whole expedition was intended to take about two months. Remembering the problems of altitude sickness on the Kilimanjaro expedition, David wanted to allow enough time to acclimatise in the Andes.

One member of the expedition was a newcomer to the club. Graham Chapman was already known to all of us as a member of the Monty Python team. A newspaper had called him and asked what he would do if he won a million pounds. Graham said he would give it to John Cleese, so that he could have an afternoon off. The newspaper thought this was a little cruel and did not print it, but they did mention instead that Graham was interested in visiting the Andes. When this was published, David called him with an invitation to come on the expedition. Graham was sensible enough not to fly a hang-glider from the top of a remote volcano when he had no flying experience, but not so sensible that he would simply buy a package holiday to South America instead, so he joined the expedition as a non-flyer. He became a popular member of the Club, and went on to participate actively in many other events.

The group left at the beginning of June 1984. They soon ran into a problem which many people have found in South America – anything that is not constantly watched, disappears. The biggest loss was about £10,000 worth of filming equipment stolen from a pickup truck five days after the group arrived. The thieves had, most likely, followed the truck since it left the airport, awaiting their chance to grab whatever they could. Cosmo Hulton was prevailed upon to hire replacements for the lost equipment.

There was a 13,000ft peak outside Quito, the capital of Ecuador, and the fliers in the group decided to use it for acclimatisation flights. Jerome Fack, whose twin brother John had been on the Kilimanjaro expedition, made several good flights. David Kirke, though, got caught in a rotor, the swirling wind which forms in the lee of a mountain, and was dashed to the ground. He was dazed by the crash and a little confused for a few days.

In his own words: *Jerome Fack*
We did a lot of training. Quito is at 10,000ft; we would drive up to 13,000 or 14,000ft, which was all part of our altitude acclimatisation, and fly. Because there were mountains, and the sun shone all the time, there was convection straight up the slope, and we could soar virtually every day. Various members of the party, like Mike McCarthy who had never been above 100ft [in a hang-glider] before, was suddenly taking off at 14,000ft and landing at 10,000ft, flying for an hour on the way down. All of the group who came to fly, did fly as much as they wanted to.

David had bought these wretched German Bergmeister gliders that packed into short bags, with a view to taking them up the mountains. They were awful things that nobody wanted to fly, people would have one flight on them and then quietly put them back in their bags and let them be. I had taken a relatively simple, light British glider, which I flew. Those mountains were really very interesting flying, you could fly from one to another and back again. The one time I really got high above them I was up at about 19,000ft, and I suddenly heard a noise – and an airliner flew past!

The team slowly assembled, and we got used to flying the gliders with cameras on, which basically wrecks them, but it was the point of the expedition. Landing with the cameras on could be interesting. David was flying one of these ghastly German gliders and had a landing which shook him severely, leaving him concussed.

The time came to make the assault on Cotopaxi. David had to show some leadership to get his mountaineers to pull together.

In his own words: *David Kirke*

Trying to get civilians to take military risks on a quasi-criminal basis, with no financial incentive, you've got to be a bit of a bastard at times…

Fourteen people set out to climb it; two got to the top, Mike Fitzroy and Mike McCarthy. The two Mikes were both ex-soldiers (Fitzroy in the Guards, McCarthy the Paras) and were physically very fit, yet they only just made it.

In his own words: *Mike Fitzroy*

I didn't go out with the rest of the group, I joined them a week or so later just before climbing Cotopaxi, so they were better acclimatised. Altitude affects people in different ways, though. Acclimatisation isn't just a question of fitness.

Cotopaxi is a dormant volcano, not spitting rocks and lava, but you can feel the heat in some places. On the climb up, we stayed in a hut at about twelve or fourteen thousand feet, and we had Graham Chapman with us, who spent the whole night chatting to porters. We kept saying, 'Just go to sleep, or we're not going to be able to do anything tomorrow.' None of us could eat anything by this stage. Our claim to fame was that we saw a UFO. It was bright, all black and white, and went up and down and left and right, and when Graham got home and was on *Wogan*, more or less all he talked about was seeing this UFO.

There was some disparity in the team. There were people like Cosmo – couch potatoes – and some who were reasonably fit, and others in between. Most couldn't go above 15,000-feet. The top was about 20,000-feet, but none of us could carry a hang-glider within a mile of that altitude. Mike McCarthy and I got within a thousand feet or so of the top. He said he wanted to stop, and sat down behind a rock. I said, 'Come on, we've got to do it,' and so we climbed the rest of the way. We had to start about 1am, before sunrise, get to the top and start down again before the ice began to melt. When we got to the top, we just stood there, and you could see sheets of mist-like ice going past us, and you could see planes landing at Quito. We didn't take a lot of pictures or anything; just stood there and went back down again. For me, it was almost a weekend affair. I'd be quite happy to go back and do it again. I was glad to drag a Parachute Regiment man to the top. It made my day.

I had this great idea half way down, to grab one of the Zap [movie] cameras and then lie on the back of my skis holding the camera and ski down. I ran straight into a rock, bust the camera and nearly broke my back.

I stayed for a week after that. We found a fantastic bridge for [bungee] jumping off. It was a deep, narrow gorge. Everyone set up cameras all around. I jumped off this thing, and it was a hairy jump, and they said, 'Sorry, we've got it wrong, you'll have to do it again…'

By a combination of physical stamina and determination, they had climbed one of the higher peaks of the Andes, a very demanding achievement and not bad going by normal standards – but in doing so, they had effectively abandoned the goal of flying hanggliders from the peak.

In his own words: *Jerome Fack*

Something was fundamentally wrong with the balance of the expedition, it didn't work as a group. It became compromised to the film, as ever; Roger Wood had an assistant who didn't want to do anything. The camp divided itself into two, three or four factions, and it became difficult to focus on what the actual event was.

Our plan on Cotopaxi was to get one glider to the top and send the fittest person. Because of the lack of cohesion, it wasn't decided which night to make the attempt, so Fitz and McCarthy went up on their own. After two or three nights in the hut, the rest of us couldn't wait any longer, so we had a go, but we were beaten back by the weather about 2,000ft from the top. The walk is strenuous, you have to use crampons and ice axes, but you're not climbing vertical faces. However, crevasses started opening up, so we had to turn back. I was going strong and hoping to fly. Subsequently I told all this to Judy Leden, and she did the flight and got it right. Her expedition was a small team equipped with little video cameras.

Having failed, we went back down to Quito, then to another volcano where we took some good flying pictures. There was not enough momentum to have another go at Cotopaxi. What we should have done is recover for a few days, eat, and get back up. But we lacked a certain purpose; it fell between a serious expedition and a sort of jolly, and it could never focus on being one or the other, which was ultimately why it failed.

Climbing Cotopaxi was a worthwhile feat in itself, at least for those who made it up there. However, the object of the trip had been hang-gliding, and the only chance of recouping some of the expedition's costs was to sell film of dramatic flights from the mountain tops. Lack of clear leadership, different levels of fitness, and many small frustrations led to divisions between members of the expedition. A splinter group began to form around the idea of going to less demanding – but still spectacular – peaks, and making flights from them. This idea found some support, but the splinter group was not cohesive enough to see it through. In the end some people, running out of money, sold their climbing gear and left Quito; two went to the beach for a week, and the expedition fell apart.

*

By August, everyone except David Kirke was back in the UK. I received a letter from him in September, postmarked the Galapagos Islands, ascribing the disappointing outcome of the expedition to team inexperience and bad weather. He felt that the stronger members of the team had been encumbered by the 'neo sub-professionals,' as Graham Chapman had described the film crew. David gave me one view of events; everyone else I spoke to gave a different view, and so I got the impression that the group which left England had never been acting as a team in the accepted sense of that word, and that the whole experience had left most of them disillusioned. It was the last of the Club hang-gliding expeditions.

9.

The Art of Debt Avoidance

*A priest is a man everyone calls 'Father', except
his children, who call him 'Uncle'.*
– Spanish proverb

Our bungee jumping displays proved to be a big crowd-
pulling attraction, for which an outdoor show organiser
was prepared to pay up to a thousand pounds on a bank
holiday weekend. David had high hopes of this becoming a regular source of income. I quite liked doing it; it could make a very
entertaining weekend out. From the start of 1983, I organised this
aspect of the business. Normally, show organisers would pay in
cash on the day, from which I would pay the costs of petrol,
consumables such as climbing rope, and so on. Those of us who did
the work got a few drinks out of it, and the rest went to the Club, i.e.
David. By this time, I was aware that the company, Dangerous
Sports Club Ltd, was wholly owned by David, and so there was
little distinction to be made between David's own money and that
belonging to the company. Few of its transactions involved large
sums, and many were in cash. This was my introduction to the
cash economy which operates in so many areas of British life.

Professional outdoor show organisers and entertainers formed
a loose-knit sub-culture, and I rapidly became familiar with many
of them. I used to meet the same arena performers at show after
show. Most of them were more serious about the business than I
was, because it was their main livelihood. One old showman trav-
elled the circuit with his son. Their equipment was a round tank of
water, about six-feet deep. At one side was a 60ft high pole, with
rungs attached and a small platform at the top. The act involved
the old man climbing the pole, setting fire to himself and diving

into the pool. He had mastered the skill of twisting as he entered the water so that he landed safely on the bottom. It was one kind of jump I had absolutely no inclination to try.

One night at a party in Oxford, I met a wild-eyed, blonde-haired party fiend called Mark Chamberlain. We hit it off straight away, somehow forming an instant, deep friendship. Mark was a photographer, who was taking a film course at the time, coincidentally taught by Roger Wood. Mark came along on my next bungee jumping show and took to it instinctively. The element of naughtiness which ran through most Club activities appealed to him, and he was soon up to his neck in all Club events. He became my regular partner in the outdoor show business, and livened up the routine aspects of the work.

Other memories of the show circuit are less warm; at least twice we were cheated by promoters, who had promised to pay us in cash on the day of the show, but then (after the performance) failed to honour their promises. It was tempting to frogmarch them to the crane, take them up a hundred feet or so, and then ask them again for the money. However, the usual reason for non-payment was a genuine shortage of cash, perhaps because not enough spectators had come. Even threats cannot conjure money out of thin air, however satisfying it might be to make them. I went to the length of getting a court liability order against one of them, which is, in theory, enforceable by bailiffs, but in practice it is fairly simple to dodge debt collectors. Recovering money from someone who is determined not to pay you, is more trouble than it is worth for a debt of just a few hundred pounds.

I was rapidly learning the art of debt avoidance from a master of the technique. David was known to many in the Club as 'Dodge' or 'Sleaze', and often referred to himself as 'Arfur', after the shady used-car dealer in the TV show, Minder. He also liked to be called 'Uncle', as in 'Uncle Dodge'. To him, I was 'Terence', a name he started using to his closer colleagues, almost as a term of affection. The Kirkespeak lexicon expanded all the time.

Whenever a line of credit became available to him, Uncle Dodge could never resist pulling it, like some piece of string, until it broke. In 1984, the company Dangerous Sports Club Ltd, which had an account (almost always overdrawn) with Barclays Bank in Soho Square, was given the useful facility of a company credit card. David and I had one each. I used mine largely to meet the expenses of doing shows.

David, however, used his Barclaycard freely for all kinds of things. He often used it to pay for food and drink from company funds. Now, a normal business pays its staff wages, from which they are expected to buy their own food. David justified his departure from standard practise by stating, correctly, that the company was never in a sound enough position to pay him a salary. He felt, then, that it was only reasonable for the firm to keep him fed and watered while he worked for it. I didn't complain, as I too ate and drank, and I believed that, ultimately, if the taxman or creditors ever got their act together and did anything, it would be done to him, not to me – and in this, I turned out to be right. David worked hard, looking for the sponsorship needed to put new ideas into action, but the combination of small, irregular income and large, regular outgoings meant the business side of the Club was on permanently rocky ground.

The Club vehicle fleet, which included useful items such as the VW pickup truck, and occasionally some more sporty cars or bikes, was seldom insured and almost never MOT'd. David himself had a driving licence from Haiti, where any sort of document could be bought quite cheaply, and later he acquired a Californian one. He had a theory that if you show foreign papers to a policeman when stopped for a traffic offence, they back off because of the complication involved in dealing with a foreign citizen. There is little point giving a speeding ticket, for example, to someone who will probably leave the country without paying it. This theory did not always work, but was only a first line of defence. Living in London, for example, you need either a fat wallet or some way of dodging parking tickets, and David's choice was the latter, for both practical and temperamental reasons.

Most people will get away with small offences if they think they can. After all, parking on a yellow line is usually a victimless crime. Where you draw the line between acceptable and unacceptable behaviour is a personal matter, and most people draw it not so very far from where the law does. David's line was drawn clear over the horizon, and we often joked that one day we would visit him in prison. Some people took a benign view of this. Hugo Spowers once said that he believed David had a commitment to the big things in life, and that possibly money was one of the little things – a charitable view not generally shared by David's other creditors.

Until the Barclaycard was withdrawn, it was a very useful thing to have, and Mahendra at the Kabana Tandoori, our favourite Indian restaurant, was always pleased to see us. We started getting the usual junk mail that comes with credit cards, including an invitation to apply for that particularly despicable status symbol, the American Express card. Well, they asked for it; we applied, and our application was supported by an impeccable reference from our accountant in Hong Kong, Mr Terence Shifter. Sadly, they smelled a rat at the last minute, possibly by checking with Barclays, and so that was one line of credit whose breaking strain we never had the chance to find out.

*

This sleaze factor was part of the reverse side of the coin. The Dangerous Sports Club of hang-gliding, bungee jumping, ski racing, high living and snook-cocking fame had another side to it, which I accommodated happily enough in those days. David was an extrovert eccentric, while I was more introverted. Working with him drew me out of myself in interesting ways. He thought like an artist, while I was logical and methodical to a fault, and we had different approaches, often complementary, to taking our risks. In business, though, neither of us could boast of any particular acumen. David often looked back wistfully on the days of the 'old firm' – the time when he, Ed Hulton, Chris Baker, and others had been able to afford to do more or less whatever they wanted to do, with no compromise imposed by sponsors. Those were the happy days before this carefree, private Club based in Oxford had turned into an unprofitable small business in London – an awkward and ultimately unsuccessful transformation. Without an adequate income from routine work like the bungee jumping displays, and without any windfall from a wealthy patron or a generous sponsor, the Club would get by on a scam here and a dodge there, relying on the enthusiasm of members to get things done. Enthusiasm, though, is not an unlimited resource, and would eventually run out. While it lasted, though, it fuelled many projects; and for me, the best was yet to come.

10.

That Rocket Fuel Feeling

'...Oh God I think I'm falling out of the sky,
I close my eyes, Heaven help me.'
– Madonna (*Like a Prayer*)

There are some events in life that stick in your mind. Some people remember hearing about President Kennedy being shot. Others, their first sexual experience, acid trip, or road accident. Most lives have some such landmarks which are permanently etched into the brain. In my own brain, my first BASE jump is etched right down to the skull.

Parachuting from a fixed object, rather than an aircraft, may have been mankind's first aerial sport. According to skydiving folklore, there is historical evidence that in the twelfth century, the Chinese amused themselves by jumping from high places, using umbrella-like devices. (I have never seen this evidence myself, but that's how it goes with folklore.) More recently, it has become a sport with a small, but very enthusiastic, following. Many of these enthusiasts were inspired by the great American film-maker Carl Boenish, who filmed some of the first parachute jumps from a cliff called El Capitan, in Yosemite National Park, California. This awe-inspiring cliff allows jumpers to make a free fall of twelve seconds before opening their parachutes. During this time, the cliff face and valley scenery fill the jumper's field of view, with rapidly changing perspective, an effect called 'groundrush'. This experience was captured by Carl Boenish's helmet-camera with such effect that just watching the film can make the viewer gasp.

These films were widely seen in the skydiving world of the late-Seventies, and soon people were jumping off bridges, skyscrapers and TV antenna towers all over the place. Boenish and his friends coined the term BASE, which stands for Building, Antenna, Span, and Earth. A jump from an object in each category would qualify you for a serially-numbered badge. (The skydiving world at that time was into numbered badges).

In 1980, it was possible to get a permit from the US National Park Service to jump off El Capitan, but the permit system was stopped after it was abused by some jumpers. Ever since then, the Park Rangers have arrested and prosecuted anyone caught jumping in Yosemite. This development symbolised the way BASE jumping lost the acceptable face it started out with, and became frowned upon by virtually every official body. It even reached the point where a skydiver found to be involved in BASE jumping was likely to be banned from their normal skydiving club. This led us to do it in secret, at night or early dawn, and to ensure that any publicity was anonymous.

I was one of those inspired by Carl Boenish's films. In the summer of 1981, when I was skydiving in California, I met several people who had jumped El Capitan. They told how, while they were falling, climbers on the rock face would yodel and bang their tin cups against the rock. The jumpers would yell back, and the walkers in the park below would join in until the valley rang with a happy chorus. Other jumps, after the ban was imposed, were made by moonlight, in total silence and tranquillity. Usually, the forbidden jumps ended with a rapid escape through the woods, but if a jumper was busted by a Park Ranger, they were in big trouble. The local court, run by magistrate Pitts, earned a reputation for throwing the book at jumpers.

In the USA, land of the very big, there are broadcasting antenna towers 2000ft high, bridges up to 1000ft high, and, of course, tall skyscraper buildings. Many of these can be jumped with little or no modification to the equipment and techniques used on ordinary aircraft jumps. All you lose by starting lower is your safety margin. In return for giving it up, you get the novelty of a jump into still air – quite different to jumping into the slipstream of an aircraft – and you can watch the tower or building go past as you fall, giving an impression of speed completely lacking on a skydive. Plus, of course, the groundrush.

Sadly, this country has very few suitably tall cliffs or towers, and British BASE enthusiasts have to make do with much lower jumps than the Americans. Britain's highest bridge, for example, is Clifton suspension bridge, just 250 feet. With so little height, parachutes must be modified to open faster, and the risks are considerably greater. I began experimenting with various parachutes I had collected for the purpose, trying different ways to get them open from crane height, about 160ft. I found that an old fashioned, round parachute would open in next to no time when I packed it in a shopping bag, which was held by an assistant who remained at the top. I used good, thick, Co-op carrier bags, with the handles in the middle. Sainsbury's bags were no good at all; this affected my shopping habits for years. I tested this shopping-bag system many times by dropping weights, before I was confident enough to jump with it myself. As the weighted harness fell, it would pull the parachute out of the bag until it reached full stretch. This took about one-and-a-half seconds. The canopy would then inflate in the next fifty feet or so. This took another couple of seconds. It would then take a further few seconds to descend to ground level, depending on the height of the crane.

I also experimented with different packing techniques. I took advice from people who had done BASE jumps before, but much of it was confused or contradictory, and I needed to do many tests to convince myself I had the right techniques. I wanted to be able to enjoy the sensations of BASE jumping without worrying too much about whether the parachute would actually open. I'm cautious like that.

In the summer of 1984, at a bungee display in Chelmsford, I completed the tests and decided I was ready to jump off the crane with my round parachute, using the shopping-bag system. Mark Chamberlain held the bag for me. I stood on the edge, looking down, oblivious to the audience below, and felt my body chemistry revving up to warp speed. When my adrenal glands reached maximum output, with great, washing waves of excitement surging round me, I jumped. Six seconds later, I landed on the grass below, so overloaded by the experience that I wasn't quite sure for some time which planet I had just arrived on. Mark was lowered by the crane and, seeing the effect the jump had on me, he wanted to try it too. Babbling gibberish, I re-packed the parachute and helped him into the harness. We went back up and I held the bag while Mark's glands did their wonderful work and propelled him over the edge. Six seconds later, he too was enjoying the rush of excitement that only BASE jumping can provide; and after that, our bungee jumping display shrank to a dull routine.

Above David Kirke was often the centre of attention

(photo credit: Mark Chamberlain)

Above David Kirke makes his first bungee jump from Clifton Bridge

Above left Confused police arrive as the first jumpers are being hauled back up

Opposite Tommy Leigh-Pemberton about to set off downhill with Nellie
Above Tim Hunt and Xan Rufus-Isaacs at the top of the slopes at San Moritz…

Above …as Tommy Leigh-Pemberton heads down on one of the simpler devices

Above The 'melonball' deflates in the Thames at Tower Bridge with David Kirke and Hugo Spowers struggling to escape

Below Martin Lyster BASE-jumping from a crane using a parachute packed in a shopping bag

Martin Lyster and Nellie
bungee jumping the
875-ft New River
Gorge bridge

(photo credit: Jean Boenish

Above Jerome Fack hang-gliding over a volcano in Ecuador
Below Martin Lyster (left) and friends go 'RW' skydiving

(*photo credit: Jim Lowe*

Top Eric, the plaster man, wore red under-pants over his most noticeable feature

Below left Xan Rufus-Isaacs fills a dull moment on the road to St Moritz

Below right Lionel Moss (left) drove the bus through the mountain passes

Above left The bus crew at the summit of the Julier Pass, an altitude record for a London bus

Right Chris Baker lowers the bus roof to go through a tunnel
    (photo credit – all this page – Eileen Haring)

Above BASE jumping often involves climbing barbed wire fences

Above Martin Lyster ready to jump the Severn pylon

Above Martin Lyster, David Kirke and Mark Chamberlain share a joke
(photo credit – all this page – Mark Chamberlain

Feeling this good, Mark and I just had to go into town together and celebrate. We picked up a man, who was also working at the showground, who asked for a ride, and we went off to paint the town. The hitch-hiker, who called himself Pat, hung around with us all evening, and developed an admiration for our VW pickup van. Later, when Mark and I had gone to sleep, he came round with a fencing stake, and thrust it into my tent. When I looked out, he beat me about the head with the stake, and took the van keys, along with some money. It was the most frightening experience of my life, to be attacked with a stake while stuck, helpless, inside a sleeping bag. Fear gripped me in a way I had never known before. BASE jumping could never arouse this feeling in me – I realised that the word 'fear' covers a whole range of different emotions, which our language is unable to describe.

Pat drove off in our van, while I woke Mark and got him to help me chase the thief. Mark, still half asleep, fell and hurt his knee. Pat had too much of a lead on us, and made it into town, where he crashed the van and ran off on foot. He then took a taxi back to the showground, where I was waiting with a policeman, and he was arrested and charged with robbery.

Mark was taken to hospital and had his knee X-rayed; nothing was broken, it just hurt. A sympathetic doctor gave him a shot of morphine and discharged him. By this time it was morning on the second day of the show, and to cheer ourselves up after this eventful night, we decided on some more BASE jumping. We also got some of our new friends from the police station to do bungee jumps in uniform.

A skydiving display team jumped into the show that day. It included a skydiving instructor called Barry, who was black. The others in the team were very disapproving of the BASE jumping, and were not at all happy when Barry asked if he could make a jump from the crane. We got him into the harness and took him up. As we rose, he gripped the hoist more and more firmly, until his hands were as white as ours. Obviously his body chemistry was going strong. I held up the carrier bag, and he jumped out. A few seconds later, he landed, and then spent about five minutes rolling helplessly on the grass, laughing convulsively. When, finally, he was able to stand up, he was grinning from ear to ear and saying it was the greatest jump of his life (and he had made thousands). Mark and I had discovered the most potent stimulant ever known. Imagine having an orgasm and a train crash simultaneously, on cocaine, with fanfares and fireworks, and you are part of the way there. And it wasn't even illegal! Well, not quite…

Soon we developed an appetite for higher jumps. Mark and I began to search out taller objects all over the country. I would drive around staring at transmitter towers (Will anyone see us? Can we climb the fence? Where could we land?) until, staring upwards one day, I drove into a hedge. The most popular BASE jumping site in the country was an antenna tower in East Anglia, near Mendlesham. It was 1100ft tall. The first time I went there, I was half way up it with a couple of friends when two other people jumped from the top. In the darkness, we had not seen them climbing. It was often like that at Mendlesham. You could have opened a snack bar there on Sunday mornings and done a roaring trade with jumpers. My main problem jumping there was climbing over the fence. I never got the hang of climbing over barbed wire without catching my clothes on the spikes. All my friends seemed to jump effortlessly over with no trouble. They would then laugh at me getting hopelessly tangled and tearing my trousers.

Mark and I paid a visit to Clifton suspension bridge early one morning, the site of the first bungee jumps and also the highest bridge in the country. We stood behind a pillar, putting our parachutes on, underneath a sign inviting anyone thinking of jumping to call the Samaritans. Our jumps went well that morning, and we came back for more; but when one of the toll collectors came out and tried to hold us back, we started to look for more isolated places.

I walked to the top of a 350 foot cliff in Cheddar Gorge, where a climber was about to abseil down. I knew it was 350ft high because he told me that was the length of his rope. He asked me how much rope I had, and I showed him my parachute. With a grin, he leaned out backwards and watched for traffic in the Gorge. When he said it was clear, I jumped. By this time I had progressed from the carrier bag system to a free-fall method, using a very large pilot chute to extract the main canopy. I jumped with the pilot chute folded in one hand, and simply threw it away to open the parachute, which made very short free-falls possible. This time, I was falling past a cliff face into a bowl-like valley, which gave a tremendous, if short-lived, groundrush. I landed by the climber's friends, who found it all very entertaining and shared their lunch with me.

It was my first cliff jump, and I realised why some other BASE jumpers regarded cliffs as the ultimate jump objects. It left a deep satisfaction long after the momentary turbo-charged rush, which gave it something more than the other jumps from cranes and bridges. My mind turned back to El Capitan.

I returned to the Gorge later with Mark and another friend, and we jumped again, but we were uncomfortably aware of the extra dangers presented by a cliff. A square parachute might open facing the cliff and fly straight into it. If this happened, the canopy would collapse and the jumper would fall down the rest of the cliff. So, we went to check out the Severn Bridge, another suspension bridge in the Bristol area, which has towers that are high enough to jump. The trouble was that these towers both stand in water, and a water landing presents a whole new set of problems. However, just beside the bridge there is a high-voltage power line, supported by pylons which are even higher than the towers of the bridge – and one of them is on land! This pylon has a convenient ladder and is particularly well designed at the top, with a long walkway across it at the very highest point, ideal for running off. It soon became our favourite jump site. All you had to do was climb the barbed wire fence (I always tore my trousers) and get to the top by first light. As long as the wind was suitable, you could jump off with a beautiful view of the sunrise over the estuary.

We were often to be found there at weekends, and it was so convenient that we were comparatively sensible about climbing back down if the wind wasn't quite right – after all, we could just come back next weekend. I brought several of my other skydiving friends along to jump there. It was never as busy as the TV antenna tower at Mendlesham, but the pylon's sloping ladder was so much easier to climb than the vertical ladder of a TV tower, and it offered a running jump, which I particularly enjoyed.

Jumping the pylon became a regular ritual. We would get up before dawn, sleepy but excited, and drive to a secluded parking place near the pylon. The ladder took about half an hour to climb, with regular pauses. We would stop just below the runway to check our kit, with the high-tension power lines buzzing and humming around us. This kit check was quite important, because we locked our parachutes closed to stop them opening accidentally during the climb up. Then we clambered up on to the runway. The difference between a running exit and a standing one is that, when you are running, you reach the point of no return before you are actually airborne. As many people have found, the anxiety of deciding to jump evaporates instantly once this point is past, leaving only the sensations of the jump to enjoy. With a running exit, you are already relaxed and fully enjoying yourself by the time you actually take to the air.

Sometimes, the anxiety crowds out the anticipation, and becomes fear. Fear isn't fun. If this happened, no-one felt embarrassed to admit it in front of their friends, who were all a little scared themselves. Nobody needs to keep up an act in this situation. You don't lose face by saying, 'I don't fancy jumping this time, I'll just take pictures and climb back down.' In fact, I have climbed down the pylon more often than I have jumped it, usually because the wind at the top was unsuitable, or because of equipment trouble, but once or twice, just because I didn't want to jump.

Once, however, we were a little late on our usual dawn schedule, and jumped in full daylight. We were seen from the nearby Severn Bridge, and the police were called out. There is a long and remote road to the base of the pylon, and while driving away from it, we saw a police car going the other way. It was later reported in the local press that the police had spent a good deal of time looking for us, and the police helicopter pilot who joined the search was so zealous that he flew under the bridge in order to examine the shoreline. This got him into trouble with the Civil Aviation Authority, who punished him – flying under bridges is very naughty. Quite what charges would have been brought against us was never made clear, but the story was sufficiently amusing that we made the press reports of it into a T-shirt design.

Our search for taller objects inevitably led us to America. In the mountainous state of West Virginia, there is a bridge over the New River Gorge which stands 875ft above the river. It is the biggest arch in the world, and the local people are very proud of it. They celebrate the opening of the bridge every year, on the third Saturday in October, by closing one side of the road and allowing people to walk along and enjoy the view. More important to us was the fact that they also allow you to jump off the bridge. In fact, BASE jumpers have, over the years, become the central attraction at Bridge Day.

Remembering the successful coverage of the ski race, we contacted the TV news company UPITN, who distribute news film via satellite, and made a deal with their sports desk to film a bungee jump from the bridge. UPITN's business was selling news, not creating it, and they were unwilling to make a direct payment as a fee for the performance. However, their consciences allowed them to pay for our air freight expenses and provide us with a thousand pounds in cash for other costs, which allowed Mark and I to go to Bridge Day, although it did not leave us with a profit. (Most of the Club was in Ecuador at the time.)

We set off with all the bungee rope we could lay our hands on, along with Tommy Leigh-Pemberton's inflatable elephant and our parachutes. Mark had not yet made a jump using a square parachute, so we spent a day up a hill in Wales, using the parachute as a hang-glider, flying around a bit and then landing it. (Paragliding, as it is called, has now become a serious sport with professional instructors and specialised equipment.) Landing a square parachute is an acquired skill which is not very difficult, but you need to get it right or you can end up hurt. At this time, Mark had not yet made a free-fall parachute jump either, as he had done all his BASE jumps using automatically-opened parachutes. At the New River Gorge Bridge, the normal parachuting technique is to hold a pilot chute in one hand, free-fall for two or three seconds, then let go of it. It then pulls out the main parachute. You then have to land on a little sandbank, which is the only open space in a valley full of trees and rocks. Mark was confident he would hit the sandbank, but I told him to be ready to land in the water if he couldn't make it.

In October 1984, we arrived in Oak Hill, West Virginia and were warmly welcomed by local people, who gave us every kind of help we needed for the bungee jump. In particular, they solved the problem of how to retrieve a jumper once the bouncing had finished, by allowing us to use the municipal tow-away truck. This was a flat-bed truck with a winch, which could haul up jumpers using a length of climbing rope.

On the day, we drove out on to the bridge and parked the tow truck near the middle. Putting all the elastic ropes together, we made a two-stranded bungee cord of about 250ft, which we hoped would stretch to about 500ft. (We normally jumped with three-stranded bungee cords, because it gives a firmer bounce, but this time length was more important than firmness.) Using a borrowed compressor, we blew up Nellie and improvised a harness for her with climbing rope. Mark jumped first, without Nellie, drawing appreciation from the spectators and a cheer from the BASE jumpers, who were leaping off at the rate of two a minute. I winched him back to the top.

Once he was back up on the bridge, it was my turn. Jumping with Nellie presented a few practical difficulties. The problem of how to launch the cumbersome, 15ft-high combination of man and elephant was solved with two greasy planks. We put these under Nellie's legs, one plank each side, so that they could pivot on the parapet. Cheerful local people were happy to oblige by lifting the back end of each plank so that Nellie could slide forward and off. West Virginians are so helpful.

I was sitting on top of Nellie as she lurched over the edge. She immediately flipped over so that I was at the bottom of the combination. Exactly the same thing had happened when Tommy had first bungee-jumped with Nellie, from a crane, the year before. This left me staring at the steelwork of the arch at disconcertingly close range, as Nellie and I accelerated downward. It takes a little over two seconds to fall past the steelwork, and I could not resist a little yell as I cleared it and saw the bright red and golden colours of the trees in the valley. Nellie slowed my fall, and so I did not bounce as low as Mark, but I was very happy with the jump, and I was sure it would please UPITN.

BASE jumpers continued to fall off the bridge at two a minute. Since most of them had not seen Nellie launched, many of them were surprised when their parachutes opened and the first thing they saw was a large pink elephant with a man in a bow tie sitting on it and waving at them. Many of these jumpers were a little uptight about making their first BASE jump, and I was delighted to be able to set them at ease with a few well-chosen remarks.

After Nellie and I had been winched back up, we had completed our obligation to UPITN and the film crew left. The item was edited down to a two minute piece and sent out that evening by satellite to UPITN's customers around the world. The staff in the London office, who had taken a chance in giving us their support, and who had become our friends, were delighted when they saw the result, partly because we were still alive, but mostly because it was a great film.

They later sent me a letter giving the estimated audience for the item. Every news station in their worldwide customer network had shown the clip, and the total viewing figure was over one billion. Had I known, as I sat on Nellie waiting to be tipped over the edge, that so many people were watching, I might have felt nervous. A quarter of the world's population had witnessed the sight of me and an elephant hanging by a rubber band. Entertaining so many people, however briefly, was something I had never dreamed of doing. Like many unplanned events in my life, it was a side-effect of my private obsession with jumping from tall objects. But to raise a billion smiles! It was a fleeting thing, not a lasting achievement, but seemed far more solid to me than my research into an obscure semiconductor material, which was the nominal purpose of my life at the time.

Mark and I had a couple of hours work ahead of us, putting away our equipment. We hurried to get the job done. The party would end and the bridge would be cleared at four o'clock, and we didn't want to be late for our BASE jumps, the real reason we had come so far. Not wanting to waste time changing, we put parachutes on over our dinner jackets and joined the queue at the exit point, ready at last to jump off the bridge the way normal people do.

BASE jumping at Bridge Day was being co-ordinated by Jean Boenish, widow of Carl the film-maker, who was killed earlier that year jumping a cliff in Norway. At the centre of the bridge, Jean had placed steps for climbing over the parapet, and she had collected money from the jumpers to pay for a rescue boat in the river below, in case anybody landed in the water. Jumpers had to wait twenty to thirty seconds following the jump before, to avoid crowding the landing site. This meant that jumpers were forming an orderly line behind the steps. Each time someone jumped, the spectators would lean over and watch to see if the parachute opened. Once it did, they all breathed out together and looked up. Meanwhile, the jumpers shuffled forward as if waiting to pay at a supermarket, making small talk with each other. The ordinariness of this behaviour had a calming effect on us. Before long, Mark was at the head of the supermarket queue. He jumped off, showing perfect technique, and threw out his pilot chute. His main parachute followed immediately, and he steered it down to the sandbank and landed, just as accurately as the more experienced skydivers. Feeling relieved at his performance, I clenched my hand around my pilot chute and followed him over the edge.

As I fell past the steelwork once again, I was free of encumbrance and more in control of events. With Nellie, I had been no more than a passenger. Now, in free-fall, my position was determined by the way I stepped off the bridge and the way I moved while falling. Not that I was trying to somersault or do any acrobatics; just falling straight down would suit me fine.

When I stepped off the rail, I was momentarily in still air, but as I gained speed downwards I felt the wind in my hair and eyes, and after a couple of seconds, I began to feel that cushion-like all-over air pressure, so familiar from skydiving. The sun glinted on the New River below me and the steep, wooded valley sides were passing up out of sight, a blur of gold and red. The shouts of the people on the bridge, the rush of the wind, and the sound of my own pulse in my ears all seemed distinct. I threw the pilot chute away and waited tensely for the parachute to open. All this only took three or four seconds, but it was definitely 'quality time', well worth the weeks of work leading up to it. I felt as if I had been crawling along in second gear for a thousand miles, and then suddenly put my foot down and shifted up into sixth.

This was what we had come for. When you get a healthy flow of adrenaline pumping round like rocket fuel in your veins, you are able, for a while, to run with all the stops out, perhaps including some stops you never knew you had. Once you have felt that way, it can be difficult to settle for living the rest of your life on half throttle; one reason regular visitors to the Real World keep coming back for more.

In this state, the mind works rapidly, and makes decisions without hesitation. A highly focused concentration is possible, with great clarity of awareness. The memory of those few seconds is still absolutely clear, years later. I felt in touch with the animal side of my nature, with instinct and reason working perfectly together. Judgement and intuition were indistinguishable from each other. Surely it is in this condition that champions win battles, prisoners break free, and athletes beat records. Whether they win the day or fall flat on their face, they will never again settle for a ringside seat in the circus of life, alongside those who never tried. And mere BASE jumpers, with no battle to win, no chains to loose, and no record to break, may still lift their spirits far above the forgettable sameness of each day in their familiar, normal world.

This can be difficult to explain to the onlooker who sees a BASE jumper as an omelette waiting to happen, and thinks it just a variation on Russian Roulette. But there is a world of difference between merely taking a random risk, and pursuing a sport in which the highest performance of mind and body is called on, and in which something important depends on that performance. We can enrich our lives this way, not cheapen them. Although we know that those who dare sometimes have to forfeit everything they have staked, we need never fear that we will die before we have ever really lived.

My parachute slammed open reassuringly hard, and I steered it down to land near Mark, on the sand bar. We hugged each other, as we often did after sharing some quality time together. We had to move aside quickly to make room for others to land, and we sat for some time watching and enjoying while the rocket fuel sensation ebbed away and left us, smiling, at the bottom of a beautiful valley, beside the swirling, dark waters of the New River. The sound of the crowd, far above, was carried away on the breeze and we could hear birds singing in the woods.

A variety of battered pickup trucks ran a jumpers' bus service between the landing site and the top. At the end of the day's jumping, we sat in one of them as it bumped and crawled its way up the valley road. Someone passed round a joint, but we didn't need any mood changing substances. Our mood was already as good as it gets. Mark and I would never forget that Day, because it was Real Life and we had shared it.

At the after-jumping party, held at the nearby Holiday Inn, several of the parachutists came up to us and remarked on the bungee jumps. At this time, bungee jumping was still a great novelty in the USA. We made a number of other friends, and I have returned to Bridge Day twice since then, sadly without either Mark or Nellie, to make more BASE jumps. The party is always a good one, running not just on the usual intoxicants, but on a little residual rocket fuel, which has euphoric and aphrodisiac qualities as well as being a stimulant.

The film of the event, which was owned by UPITN, has been very widely sold, and is still selling today, twelve years on. If only I had a penny for each time it has been shown, I would be a rich man – sadly, no such deal was on the table. I have seen clips of the film on aeroplane inflight entertainment, and even in a TV programme about a commercial bungee jumper from New Zealand, A J Hackett. This film turns up at odd times and places; the strangest occasion yet being reported by two bungee jumping friends of mine who recently got married. Their honeymoon was in Thailand, trekking in the forest and riding on an elephant. It was a great holiday, and at the end of it they spent a night in

Bangkok. They had a TV in their room, and sure enough, the film of Nellie and I jumping came up. Somehow, my ghostly image had followed them to Thailand, and I even had an elephant too.

We had not been home long when the Ecuador expedition returned. They were mostly unhappy and considerably poorer, and I could only be glad I had turned down the invitation to go. Mark and I had obviously had a lot more fun. David Kirke stayed on in South America, returning much later with stories of a mysterious encounter with a fugitive Nazi war criminal. He was fond of showing the name of this Nazi, Sassens, in the *Book of Lists* under the heading Ten Most Wanted Nazi War Criminals (Sassens was number eight). He did not go into any detail about how they had met, or why. Perhaps it took his mind off the disappointment of the hang-gliding expedition.

*

Do you sometimes get the feeling that almost everyone else knows something you don't? After years of being told I was crazy, I slowly got used to the idea that one of the basic rules of life (which I had somehow failed to grasp) was that, 'People in their right minds don't jump out of perfectly good aircraft.' Well, it wasn't a big problem. Most of the time I could pretend to be in my 'right' mind. When actually skydiving, I could be my real self among friends, which was comforting and reassuring. But then it dawned on me that I had also completely missed another of the basic rules of life, one which even the other skydivers had sussed: 'People in their right minds don't jump off cliffs, cranes, and bridges.' There weren't many of us who hadn't twigged that one, so we didn't meet each other very often, and missed out on reassurance. It made me sad that much of the opposition to BASE jumping came from other parachutists – the very people I had thought were on my side. Some of them were sympathetic, in a hushed voice – but the official line was one of stern condemnation.

Of course, skydiving takes place on regulated airfields, under the control of instructors and officials, while BASE jumping is done without controls and by people who don't always know what they are doing. When BASE jumpers are killed – the first one to be killed in the UK, Frank Donellan, died in 1981 jumping from a block of flats in London – the distinction between BASE jumping and skydiving is often too obscure for reporters to grasp. The British Parachute Association (BPA) feared that BASE jumpers would tarnish the reputation of skydiving. This attitude, despite a lack of evidence to justify it, led to BASE jumpers being stigmatised and forced underground, where we formed a lively but secretive sub-culture within the parachuting community. Legitimate skydiving, meanwhile, continued to enjoy a boom in the numbers of people wanting to try a jump; it seemed that neither the occasional BASE jumping incident, nor the more frequent incidents in routine skydiving, had the feared effects on public or official acceptance of the sport.

I did not want my BASE jumping activities to get me into trouble with the BPA. The difficulty was that I was making some BASE jumps in public. For a time I tried using a stage name, but it didn't work, and the chief instructor of my local skydiving club got to hear about it. When I showed up at the airfield after I got back from Bridge Day, I was told to leave the club, and ended up jumping elsewhere for a few years. Today the antagonism has mellowed, and it is no longer a problem. But I have never lost the urge to jump El Capitan.

One day…

11

There always seemed to be some sort of party going on...

'It's just *not fun* to have exciting thrills when
you're scared. Take the heroes of the *Iliad*, for
instance – they really had some exciting thrills,
and were they scared? No. They were drunk.
Every chance they could get. And so am I, and
I'm not going out there and have a horrible car
wreck until someone brings me a cocktail.'

– P J O'Rourke, *How to Drive Fast on Drugs While
Getting Your Wing-Wang Squeezed and Not Spill
Your Drink*

When I first met him, David lived in Oxford, but shortly
afterwards he moved to live with his girlfriend Miranda
at her house in Fulham. The house was in Shorrolds
Road, and we called it Shoddy. It was filled with equipment and
usually with people, and its long-suffering owner put up with a
great deal – she was not generally an active participant herself in
Club activities, although she helped a lot behind the scenes and
cheerfully allowed her home to be overrun. Shoddy had a convenient off-licence within staggering distance, and there was an
excellent Indian restaurant, the Kabana Tandoori, nearby in the
Kings Road. There were several memorable parties at Shoddy,
which was a terraced house with a back yard just big enough to set
up a barbecue. The front room was decorated with a large mural
painting which completely filled one wall, showing an exotic
tropical landscape. It was painted by an artistic lodger who was
unable to pay his rent with money.

In the mid-Eighties, Shoddy was the nerve centre of most Club activities, and I spent a lot of time there, mostly in a spare room at the top of the house which served as an office. David hired a succession of assistants, who in his vaguely patronising way he referred to as Girl Fridays. They were cheerful, enterprising, over-worked, and paid – when there was any – in cash. Eileen Haring was Girl Friday around the time of the third ski race in 1985, and proved invaluable in organising things. Like her successor, Nina Knox-Peebles, she made up for a wide range of inadequacies on the part of David, myself, and the others.

Most of the equipment for bungee jumping and other activities was normally stored in the cellar at Shoddy. With huge coils of rubber, harnesses, clips, ropes, assorted specialised clothing, and various odd-shaped, unidentifiable pieces of junk, it often resembled something between a fetishist's playroom and an outdoor sports jumble sale. When I was arranging and performing the Club's bungee jumping displays, I frequently came to Shoddy to collect the bungee equipment and take it to the show location, either in my own grotty old car or, preferably, in the Club's VW pickup truck. This truck could carry half a dozen people along with a lot of equipment, and was ideal for the sort of jobs we were doing.

From this base we tried for years to arrange sponsorship deals, TV work, and expeditions. Our ambitions ran as far as a Hollywood movie production. The results, though, were disappointing, at least financially. Running anything in London costs money, and the Club was a business without a regular, steady income. When we did find work, we almost always underpriced ourselves.

At one party at Shoddy in 1984, we held a wine tasting with the aim of choosing a Dangerous Sports Club own-label wine. By arrangement with wine merchant Tim Mason, we tasted a variety of reds and whites, looking for one of each that we could afford in reasonable quantities, but which we would not be embarrassed to have our name on. We made our selection, and bought fifty cases of each – or perhaps 'ordered' would be a better word[1]. The red wine was called 'Commanderie des 4 Reines' (I forget what the white was, I didn't like it), and when the first batch arrived we looked forward to selling it fairly quickly. It had a label depicting a ski-jumping waiter flying across an Alpine scene, with the name

[1] This phrase was originally used to describe this transaction by Radio 4 reporter Giovanni Ulleri.

of the Club across the top. The bulk price was a little under £3 a bottle, and we hoped to knock it out for £3.50 to Club members and their friends, which seemed a reasonable mark-up. How touchingly naive we were.

It quickly became obvious that Club members and assorted hangers-on were far more interested in drinking the wine than in paying for it. An increasingly irritated Tim Mason often visited Shoddy to ask for payment. Whenever he came round, he found, in his own words: 'There was always some sort of party going on, at which more wine was being drunk than sold.' If anything this was an understatement. The wine was being drunk in industrial quantities, and next to none of it was being sold.

Although we were quaffers rather than connoisseurs of wine, several of us found the Club plonk disappointing, remembering how good it had seemed at the tasting; somehow, it tasted very ordinary when knocked back by the gallon. The unfortunate Mr Mason was never fully paid, a penalty usually meted out to anyone rash enough to extend credit in David's direction. I still have a bottle tucked away; I wonder whether it has improved with age.

Although our social events always involved opening bottles, not all of us drank like Oliver Reed; in fact, Graham Chapman was completely teetotal, following his recovery from alcoholism some years before. Having Graham in the Club sometimes created interesting situations on account of his celebrity status. For example, in 1984, when the Ethiopian famine was very much in the public eye, he was involved in celebrity fundraising efforts, like the Band Aid record. In November 1984, there was a concert at the Albert Hall, which Graham compéred, in which about a dozen well-known bands played. We were invited to provide some kind of diversion during the interval.

Our first thought was an indoor bungee jump, but when we had a look at the Hall, we realised the sounding-boards suspended from the dome, like huge inverted mushrooms, would get in the way. The dome itself has an inner and an outer skin, and when we went up in between the two, we found that, at the top, there is a large opening in the inner skin through which you can look right down to the floor nearly 200ft below. In this opening, there are some structural steel bars which meet in the centre, covered with a welded grid so that you can walk on the bars without slipping through. A hatch in the grid provides a way to get down into the hall, and there are several winches for hoisting the sounding boards and lighting equipment. An idea suggested itself straight away; we could lower Nellie between the sounding-boards, with one of our number dressed as Santa Claus, all the way to the floor. The winch gear was perfectly adequate to bear the weight, but is intended for equipment rather than people, so the Hall employee in charge, Mr Cottrell, said we couldn't do it with a person, just the elephant.

On the day of the show, we inflated Nellie on the floor and made up a harness for her from rope and webbing. Lowering the winch cable, we attached Nellie and raised her to the top of the Hall, just beneath the grid. I went out to rent a Santa Claus costume, and we were all set.

The show got off to a good start, and towards the end of the first half, we left our seats and climbed the back stairs to the top of the dome. I put the costume on over my harness, and lowered myself through the hatch. Hanging from the steel bars, I swung across to Nellie and attached myself to her. While the last band of the first half played (which was my favourite reggae group, Aswad), Nellie and I were gently lowered to just above the level of the mushrooms. A few people in the highest boxes saw us and peered curiously, but I was in shadow and must have been hard to recognise as Father Christmas on an elephant.

In a book I read as a young child, the Albert Hall is used as a mould for the world's largest jelly. Looking down on it, I had to admit that this really wouldn't be a bad idea. It contains a very large empty space, and the people are all stuck to the sides, many of them barely able to see the stage. I was pleased that we were going to use the space, in some entertaining way. If nothing else, I was getting an interesting view of Aswad.

As the applause began to fade into a rustling of papers and people started heading for the bars and toilets, the others started lowering me into the arena. People began seeing Nellie and waving at us, and I waved back. When I reached floor level, I detached myself and climbed down off Nellie's back. Nellie began her slow ascent back up to mushroom level. I was carrying a large box of sweets, which I began handing out to children in the audience. I am not naturally inclined to regard children as cute, appealing and desirable, and normally keep them at arms length or further, but that night, for the first time, I found their responses heartwarming (I had never played Santa before). The response of the Albert Hall staff, though, was rather different.

I made my way slowly towards the only exit I could see which was not manned by any burly men with murder in their eyes. Once through, I made a dash for it and hid in a phone box. Fortunately, it had a proper solid door, and so I was able to pull off my costume un-noticed, feeling a bit like a down-market Clark Kent. I came out clutching a carrier bag containing the fancy dress.

Heading back up to the roof, I met David, Miranda, Xan Rufus-Isaacs and Tim Hunt, who had by this time winched Nellie back up to roof level, and were coming down again. We took our seats for the second half, which commenced with Graham, the compére, asking the audience for contributions to the appeal. I was a little surprised when David got up and handed over a cheque, drawn on the Club's account, for £500; a grand gesture indeed, given the size of the Club overdraft. Still, I expect the Ethiopians needed it more than Barclays Bank. We were then treated to the Band Aid song 'Do They Know It's Christmas?' sung by a composite group, including the songwriters Midge Ure and Bob Geldof, and several of the other pop stars who had recorded it. The spirit of goodwill stopped there, however, and as the audience left, the Hall staff were out in strength to stop us recovering our equipment. They stood in our way, shoulder to shoulder across the stairs, and threatened to call a policeman to arrest me.

Fortunately Xan, who is a barrister, was able to explain to Mr Cottrell that they had no right to do this, whatever rules I may have broken, and that dire legal consequences would follow if they deprived us of our property by threatening the use of force. He made it sound like armed robbery worth a fifteen-year stretch. Whether or not all this was true, they weren't quite sure, but in the end we were allowed to recover Nellie, and proceed to the performers' party at a West End night club.

I had been looking forward to this, since I am not a regular at West End night clubs and had never partied with rock stars before – only heard the stories, which sounded promising. Sadly, I found that these rich, famous and talented people were actually quite well behaved. There was little sign of either sex or drugs, and the rock and roll was pre-recorded. It was still an enjoyable party though, if a bit restrained compared to my more exotic expectations.

Good parties often seemed to end in unexpected ways in those days. Mark and I did a bungee show at Cheltenham in the summer of 1985, which went down well with the crowd, although we were cheated of our payment by the organiser. Chris Baker came to the show, and I had the pleasure of arranging his first bungee jump – over six years after he had invented the sport. I had not realised until then that Chris, who had missed the first jump at Clifton, and got his equipment tangled at the Golden Gate, had not personally experienced the sensation he had given to many others; to him, once it had been done by someone else, it lost most of its appeal. He enjoyed it all the same, in his calm and reserved manner, and did another jump straight away. After the show, Mark, Eileen, and I drove down to Devon for a party held by Wally Blacker, who was the first Club member to make an intentional 'splashdown' bungee jump into the river Avon, from the Clifton Bridge. He was staying in a magnificent country house a few miles outside Exeter. It was a big party which went on all night, with plenty of sex and drugs for those interested, as well as live rock and roll. By morning, there were heaps of bodies all over the house and garden. David Kirke arrived from London about dawn, driving a brand new Alfa Romeo Cloverleaf. He wandered into the house and found me in a pile of party debris.

'Wake up, Martin, come and have a spin in my new car,' he said, prodding me into semi-consciousness. I followed him outside, while he explained that he had scored this car, largely on the strength of his favourable reviews of it in *Men Only* magazine, and that he had just collected it and driven down from London to Exeter. Indeed it had only 300 or so miles on the clock, and was very smart – comfortable interior, electric windows, good radio and so on. I wasn't quite sure why David wanted someone in my condition – uninsured, hung-over and bleary-eyed – to drive his brand new car, but I think it was the excitement of showing off a new toy. I preferred not to take the wheel straight away as I was still having some difficulty working out which way was up, so I got in the passenger seat and David invited me to sit back and enjoy the ride. He engaged first gear, revved up and dropped the clutch. The front wheels ejected a fine spray of gravel; but once they found some grip, we were pressed firmly back in our seats as the car shot forward. We were heading straight towards a mature oak, one of several fine specimens of that species in the grounds. I felt quite confident that once the heady rush of intoxicating acceleration was over, David would steer away from it and out towards the open road.

We hit the tree at sufficient speed to write off the car. The offside front quarter was caved right in, where it had hit the left side of the tree. The car rolled over on to its roof and lay in the drive. The engine cut and there was a gentle tinkling sound of broken glass. I was distracted by a trickle of wine dripping past my face in the wrong direction. Once I worked out that we were upside down, I tried the door, but it was bent and would not open. David began to swear.

I wriggled into a kneeling position. The roof was slightly closer to the seat than it had been before the crash, and there was little headroom. Sad to say, the electric windows would not open, and although the windscreen had popped out in one piece on impact, we could not get out that way either, because the car lay nose down. For about ten minutes we were stuck.

'A drastic way to empty the ashtrays, and they weren't even full,' I said, in a sorry attempt at cheering up David, who had turned uncharacteristically quiet.

'Can you smell petrol?' he replied, not quite appreciating (as I could) the irony of making such a remark while lighting a pipe.

In this manner we kept our spirits up until a group of party-goers came upon us. At first they thought the upside down car was part of the decoration, like the crashed wheelchairs which were tastefully scattered around following some experiments with elastic rope the night before. When we asked them to help, they thought about it for a while, then rolled the car over on to its wheels. Upright again, David and I could get out through the broken sun roof. David lay down beside the car, covered himself with a blanket, and went to sleep; I went back to rejoin the party.

The car was left where it lay, and eventually was towed away and scrapped. Amazingly, when David admitted that he had written it off within 24 hours of delivery, Alfa's response was to give him another. Apparently several members of the board of Alfa's UK distributor had done much the same, although not usually quite so promptly. The new one was promptly delivered, and we took it out to Birmingham, for our next event.

We had been hired to fill three slots in a childrens' Saturday morning TV show called *The Saturday Starship*, and as we had to prepare our performance at 6am, we were accommodated overnight at a hotel, and entertained in a nearby nightclub. The *Starship* programme was so awful it was almost consciously self-parodying. The gormless presenters wore silver 'spacesuits' and introduced a procession of minor celebrities and pop videos; I had the pleasure of meeting glam-rock idol Noddy Holder from Slade, between jumps. We were scheduled to perform a bungee jump and a catapult (flinging someone upwards) using a crane in the TV station car park. Following this, I offered to make a BASE jump, largely to try out a new piece of equipment I had obtained for making very low free-fall jumps. To reassure the director (and myself), I made a last-minute test of the equipment by dropping the parachute with a sandbag in the harness, which narrowly missed the new Alfa, landing heavily beside the driver's door. After quickly repacking the parachute, I made my jump, which was the closing item of the show, dressed once again as Father Christmas, giving a loud cry of: 'Ho, Ho Ho!'

I could hardly believe it when the presenter told the audience not to try it at home. Well, if they wanted to, and they happened to have a 200-foot crane and a parachute lying around, would they really be put off by some cretin in a spacesuit telling them not to? I left, wondering whether repeated orders not to attempt anything hazardous (which covers most difficult and worthwhile things) would produce a generation whose preferred response to a challenge would be to avoid it, or to panic, rather than to take it on and overcome it. Then I realised with dismay that I was becoming old and pompous.

*

There are people in adventurous sports who cherish the delusion that they are members of some kind of daring elite. I have met any number of skydivers who believed that they were marked out as different from (and, by implication, superior to) the common herd who do not choose to hurl themselves into space every weekend. This attitude is reinforced by a private language which includes such unflattering words as 'whuffo' (short for 'Whuffo you jump out them airplanes?') meaning non-skydivers. David Kirke shared this sort of elitist view, on top of ordinary social snobbery, often making derogatory remarks about the kind of people who live in Bromley and have nine-to-five jobs. However tempting it might be to ego-trip in this way, I could never regard the Club as any kind of elite. There were so many damaged personalities in it that I came to see it as a sort of half way house between the Keystone Kops and Alcoholics Anonymous. As for myself, within the BASE jumper there still lurked a Northern Chemist, who would probably emerge on top in the end. For the Club as a whole, the farcical, Keystone Kops element was to grow stronger in everything we subsequently did on our pilgrimage from artistic licence to chaotic irrelevance. Those whose path through life took them to Bromley needn't feel they missed too much.

12.

Hamlet (without the Prince of Denmark)

'If there isn't a God, someone's got an
awful lot of explaining to do.'
– Xan Rufus-Isaacs

I believe that the oldest known ski was found near Høtig in Sweden. It is short and wide, a design which is regarded today as a great innovation. It is estimated to be 4,500 years old. In all these millennia of skiing, though, it seems it did not occur to anyone to mount a double-decker bus on skis, until the innovative and audacious Xan Rufus-Isaacs did so for our third – and as it turned out, last – ski race, held on 19th March 1985.

Our ideas and devices had continued to get bigger and better. Chris Baker once said that the ski races were a tremendous surreal display, probably the most successful to be placed before the public in our time, but as a way of getting a serious buzz, they left a certain amount to be desired, and logistically, they were chaotic. The third time round, we set out to overcome these drawbacks with the biggest, fastest machines yet, more sponsorship money, a steeper slope and a better organising team. The work involved in preparing the race was intense; by the time we left for Switzerland, Eileen, David and I had barely slept for a week. Our sponsor was the British distributor of an Italian sparkling wine called Gancia, who paid £8,000.

We had to make a couple of promotional appearances for the sponsor before the event itself. This involved dragging our machinery into silly places and smiling at cameras. The most tiresome appearance was at the Trocadero shopping centre in Piccadilly. In the spirit of the mid-Eighties, this small imitation of an American mall was filled with shops selling the fashion items of the time – striped shirts and braces, mobile phones, filofaxes and all the other absurdities of yuppie posing. We brought in some of the smaller ski devices and arranged them in an 'exhibition', which uninterested shoppers had to stumble around to get from the specialist sausage shop to the organic cosmetics franchise. The effort it involved for us was an irritating distraction from the real work of getting the machines built and shipped. An annoying irrelevance it may have been for us and the shoppers, but it was part of the sponsorship deal. We had to suffer for our art.

This year, as well as the usual collection of wheelchairs, bath-tubs and so on, we had a Venetian gondola, a full-scale 'Red Baron' Fokker, and a life size, accurate replica of a cruise missile. Also, there was a giant model of the sponsor's product, a Gancia bottle, big enough to carry two people inside. All of this had to be prepared and stowed in the container which our truck driver Billy Hannant would drive to St Moritz. Some of these items had been crafted by Steve Smithwick in his scenery workshop near Waterloo, while others had been built in the usual way in various backyards and garages around the country.

The largest item could not be sent in a container, but fortunately it was capable of getting there under its own power. Stalwart Club member, rugby player, barrister and hedonist, Xan Rufus-Isaacs had decided to enter a double-decker London bus into the race. Everyone was very enthusiastic about this, and the entire Dangerous Sports Club wanted to be aboard when it went down the slope. There was even some premature argument over who could sit in the front seats on the top deck. The Swiss were informed and raised no objection. A few people wanted to arrange a series of bus stops down the hill, at which bowler-hatted passengers would attempt to leap aboard as the bus went past, but this idea was obviously ridiculous. However, we were all convinced that a skiing double-decker bus would be the outstanding work of surrealist performance art of our time; pictures of it would appear in publications around the world, and it would be one of the great, lasting images of the 1980s, just like the picture of Aldrin standing on the moon from the 1960s. (None of us could think of a great, lasting image from the 1970s).

Just getting the bus out there involved endless work. The paperwork for the ski races had never been straightforward. The documents involved in exporting such goods were very complicated. For example, we had to pick up and carry back all the wreckage after the race; if the devices that got trashed had been thrown away in St Moritz, they would be classed as permanent exports, and would be taxable. If we returned them from Switzerland to the EC, however badly damaged, they were only temporary exports. We had to prepare a list on which each item was detailed: *One pink elephant, inflatable; one desert island, plus gramophone; seven wheelchairs, ski-mounted; one bed, four poster...* We submitted the list to the authorities in advance, so that they could issue the necessary carnet. One of our problems was that, until people actually showed up to load their devices into the container, we never knew exactly what was coming. Telling the necessary lies to the customs officer was quite easy given that most items on the list were unrecognisable from their descriptions.

These sort of problems were repeated for the bus and its skis. A near-catatonic state set in when we discovered that Switzerland does not admit vehicles over 4m (about thirteen-feet) high because of the many low tunnels and overhead cables. A double-decker stands just over fourteen-feet high. We ended up finding another bus, which had already been modified to meet the Swiss height requirements. The roof was mounted on hydraulic rams, and if the upper deck windows were taken out, the roof could be lowered until it was under the 4m limit. Lowering the roof was a fairly simple task and reminded me of those old horror movies in which the ceiling is slowly brought down, impaling the victim on spikes. (There were no spikes in the bus, though I tried to impro-vise some.) Also, a steel shutter had been fitted to the platform at the back of the bus, allowing it to be locked up.

The night before we left, the bus was involved in another promotional appearance, on London local TV. The programme was imaginatively entitled *The Six O'Clock Show*, and had organ-ised a competition among its viewers. The prize was a trip for two to St Moritz to watch the ski race, and participate if desired. The winners were selected on the show, and were sent off on the bus, as if they were going to Switzerland that night, at the end of the show. Naturally, once we turned a corner and were out of sight of the cameras, we stopped and dropped off the winning pair, who flew out two days later. They did not seem particularly interested in the ski race, which was a pity as I am sure some viewers could have been found who would have got more involved in the event.

The bus, which cruised at a stately forty miles per hour, had to leave a few days early. The crew were Xan, Chris Baker, myself,

Mark Chamberlain, Eileen Haring, a genuine licensed bus driver called Lionel Moss, and Eric, the plaster man. Eric was a Club member in the same sense as Nellie the inflatable elephant; although not possessing the priceless gift of consciousness which distinguishes us from the brutes, Eric and Nellie nevertheless participated in many exciting sports. Eric was a life-size humanoid made of plaster, with eyeballs that moved like those of an Action Man; a small mouth-hole which would just hold a cigarette; and last but certainly not least, an enormous erection, which could be moved from behind his back. We had rescued him from the National Theatre in one of their occasional clear-outs. I don't know what they needed him for; the mind boggles.

Eric took part in the ski race, and in later years he made several bungee jumps. He even made a BASE jump, at a show in Belfast; but I am sad to relate that his parachute failed to open in time and he 'went in', as we say, losing a leg or two. (As a morbid experiment in crowd behaviour, I had prepared his parachute so it wouldn't work; and the crowd cheered even louder than usual when Mark made a more successful jump a few minutes later). Eric was repaired following his hard landing and subsequently accompanied us on many more Awaydays.

The double-decker London bus, with the open platform at the back, narrow staircase, and distinctive red livery, is a design classic and a national icon. It is also a cold, slow and uncomfortable way to go to Switzerland, but the journey was delightful in spite of these drawbacks. After a couple of days on the road, we reached Reims, in France's champagne-making region. We parked in the centre of town, and went to look for a funnel for diesel oil. The town fire station obliged, and the whole crew of *pompiers* came out to look. Chris drove one of their fire engines around, while they took turns in the bus. Showing traditional French welcoming spirit, they got out a case of champagne to toast our success. This was more than welcome, because we had limited amounts of drink on board. We had bought the usual duty-frees, but apart from that all we had were a dozen cases of Gancia. This stuff is a bit of an acquired taste, and we had not managed to acquire it despite several heroic attempts. It came in handy for bribing various minor officials at Calais who weren't satisfied with our paperwork.

Rumbling sedately across Europe in such good company was a real traveller's delight. The bus itself was not set up for sleeping in, although sometimes one of us would do so if we felt insecure about leaving it unattended. Eric was dressed as a bus conductor, or at least partially dressed. His most noticeable feature was generally covered by a pair of red Y-fronts, although its prominence attracted a number of double-takes, particularly from ladies. The journey took four or five days, which in these times is too slow even for hitch-hikers, who mostly passed up our offers of a lift and waited for something a bit faster to come along. At least, I think that's why they turned us down.

To pass the time, we amused ourselves in many ways. Chris and Mark liked to stand up at the front and dodge bridges by ducking at the last moment. Eileen, Eric and I liked to sit on the rear platform making conversation as the world passed by. Xan was usually at the front with Lionel, navigating. Xan is a tall and imposing man with a habit of giving a deep-voiced chuckle when about to commit socially unacceptable acts. His entry of a bus in the ski race was typical of his extravagant and original sense of humour. I don't think anyone who met us on that journey could have mistaken us for Cliff Richard on another *Summer Holiday*; somehow, we lacked that wholesome atmosphere.

The route across the Alps to St Moritz had given me problems the year before when I drove out in my Cortina, loaded up with three people and an elephant. Then, I was stuck in first gear for forty miles over the Julier Pass, which at 7,500ft is the highest point of the journey. However the bus was made of sterner stuff, and had few difficulties in the mountains. It tended to overheat, which we cured by pouring cold liquid over the radiator. At the summit of the Julier Pass there was a sign declaring the altitude, and since this was a record for a London bus, Lionel wanted the sign as a souvenir. The bus chose this moment to overheat, and we were out of water, so we found a use at last for our spare Gancia.

We were passing through Cuntur, about 100 miles from St Moritz, when two cars containing PR people from the Gancia distributor's advertising agency caught up with us. Judging by their collection of partners and skis, they were treating it as a chance for a skiing holiday at the clients' expense. They followed the bus for some time, and we wondered when they would decide they had had enough of our stately pace and leave us behind. They did so shortly after Xan made an obscene gesture at them from the rear platform of the bus, soiling a Gancia T-shirt in the process. Our disrespect for the paraphernalia of sponsorship did not extend to the sponsor himself, however. The owner of the firm,

Max Gancia, had driven up from Italy to attend the race. He turned out to have a good sense of humour and none of the tacky mannerisms of the PR consultants.

At St Moritz, we stayed once again in the Chantarella hotel. This was an old building with high ceilings, creaking floorboards and one bath per landing. When you wanted a bath, you had to call a maid to run it for you. In other words, it had some character, but was not very well suited to the modern ski hotel trade, which calls for effective heating, en suite bathrooms, reliable hot water and so on. I believe we were put up there because it would matter less if we caused damage; the hotel was due for modernisation later that year anyway. In the end, the only damage I can recall was a bed being thrown out of a window, and some strawberry jam left on the ceiling when Mike Fitzroy set off a detonator in a jampot, after a cheeky waiter had complained about our repeated indoor use of explosives.

The race itself looked like being our best yet, but things soon took a bad turn. The local authorities, on the actual morning of the race, refused us permission to put the bus on the slope. Without their help, we could never hope to move it, since we had counted on using their piste-rolling tracked vehicles to tow the bus around on the snow. We spent some time looking for an alternative slope which would be more acceptable, but could not get agreement anywhere. Some very bad feeling was building up. The Swiss front man, Martin Berthod, took a lot of stick from us, but the decision was final: no bus. After all the work that had gone into it, we were more than a little pissed off. The Swiss treated us as second-class citizens because we made a bit of noise and mess; that we were used to. But to be subject to arbitrary last minute restrictions like this was intolerable. As artists, we found it completely unacceptable that they should limit our expression. It was an outrageous denial of every Englishman's right to drive his bus down the mountain of his choice.

In his own words: *Xan Rufus-Isaacs*

I remember we went out on a reconnaissance to St Moritz. That was the year we decided to go for the steeper slope, which in hindsight was an appalling mistake, but there's no accounting for taste. I think the slope we used the first two years, was, well... we wanted to rev it up a bit. I remember talking to Martin Berthod about the bus, and he was saying what an excellent idea it was, and we joked about making a jump for it. There was no doubt in any of our minds that they approved the bus, and which slope we were going to do it on and all that. So then we went ahead and got the bus, and the skis, and spent a few bob on it.

Early on the morning of the race, we were having breakfast and Martin Berthod turned up and said that his boss Hans Peter had vetoed it on the grounds that there wasn't a proper braking mechanism in place, which indeed there wasn't, but there was enough of a run-off slope. In any event one of the ideas was to turn the thing over if it looked as if it was getting dodgy – you turn it sideways to the hill, and the thing's going to tip over, which is going to make it interesting for the people on the top deck.

Anyway, it was not to be. I took a swing at Martin Berthod in the foyer of the Chanterella, and went down to see Hans Peter in the tourist office and he said, 'I've decided you can't do it; Martin Berthod didn't have authority to give permission.' Basically I thought it was some sort of political thing, with it being a bad environmental image to have the bus on the slopes – particularly if it couldn't be retrieved – and an election the following week.

The race went ahead without the bus. It was still the best ski race we had yet held, but seemed like Hamlet without the Prince of Denmark. Another machine was out of the running for technical reasons (the operating theatre, for which I had spent a good deal of time obtaining three gallons of AB rhesus positive), but all the other devices went ahead. The cruise missile was probably the fastest, at least by the time it reached the bottom of the piste, and it failed to stop. The two passengers, Steve Smithwick and his assistant Tom Brunson, suddenly realised they weren't going to stop, and they huddled inside the polystyrene body of the missile. They disappeared from sight and the crowd at the bottom of the run drew in a collective breath.

In his own words: *Steve Smithwick*

We were really pleased with our cruise missile. We had really researched it, we had got loads of pictures of Tomahawk missiles, and all the dimensions and so on out of Jane's, it was a very accurate model. It had seats, but otherwise it was exactly right. We didn't put brakes in, because I thought last time, it was a very fast slope, but things either smashed up or hit a snow bank, and nothing really reached the bottom, so a brake was just a waste of time. I didn't bother with steering either. I really didn't think that it was going to go very far. Tom and I got in, and we hadn't tried it or anything, obviously, and we went off expecting to roll down the hill. We got past the bit where everybody normally crashed, where Graham and Eric's boat crashed, carried on going and got to the end. You came over a sort of hill at the end, and there were huge crowds down there, cheering, so we eventually came right to the bottom and came on to a flat area, so we put our arms up thinking we'd done it.

What we didn't realise immediately was that we were still gaining speed. We could see this snow bank ahead that was supposed to stop us, and it was just like a ski jump, we went straight over and disappeared. I can remember going over it and hearing all the crowd go, 'OH!'. We went down an off-piste slope for a couple of hundred yards into a row of trees, and I remember looking at these trees and laying down inside the thing. We hit a tree head on, we must have been doing at least 50mph. The missile, which was 24ft long, was solid polystyrene, and that just completely disintegrated, soaking up the impact. I remember my head slamming against the tree, and Tom hitting the tree, and being awake while he was unconscious. I had this picture of Tom's mother at Customs and me wheeling him through in a chair. Then I could hear lots of skis. I thought they had come to take us up, but it was a load of photographers. Five minutes later a couple of guys with a stretcher took Tom up. We were so shaken, because these photographers showed us that twenty yards beyond the trees was a sheer drop into the town. If we hadn't hit the tree we would have gone whistling over and launched into space.

For the first time, there was an outside entry in the ski race. A couple of Germans showed up with a heavily modified Citroen 2CV. It had dustbins for wheels, an elaborate paint job, and a sculpture on the front resembling a giant chicken's head. It went down well, at a good speed and even under some control. Graham Chapman, Xan, Eric and I went down in a gondola, which overturned and broke into matchwood about two thirds of the way down, interrupting an absorbing conversation on the effects of nitrous oxide. Somehow, when a breakable device crashed, it always splintered into tiny pieces, and when a metal device crashed, it would be bent and twisted by the force of the crash. People, though, if thrown clear, were always perfectly all right, getting up and laughing about it straight away. Injuries only happened when a person was completely inside their device and unable to separate from it when it overturned.

The coverage was, as usual, very good and I believe the sponsor was happy, although the film broadcast on Italian TV showed Max Gancia and Steve Smithwick on the slope with some of the devices, with Steve wearing an adjusted T-shirt. Instead of the slogan, *I went down at St Moritz with Gancia*, it bore the statement *I went down at St Moritz with Ganja*.

After the race, I went home with Billy Hannant in his truck. Billy, built like a bear and with dense orange hair, had spent the time in St Moritz screaming around on a four-wheel Yamaha 'bike' which was surprisingly good on snow and ice. Billy drove his truck back to the Channel more or less non-stop, and I spent most of the trip in the bunk of his cab nursing a sore eye. Meanwhile, for Xan and Chris, getting the bus home was a long, hard slog:

In his own words: *Xan Rufus-Isaacs*

We didn't really want to drive it back, if we could avoid it, so we tried to find if anybody in Switzerland wanted a second hand London bus. We got quite a bit of publicity for it, and found out that, no, nobody in Switzerland did want a rather beaten up old second hand London double-decker bus, even if it was a convertible. Chris and I drove back to Calais non-stop, got it on a ferry, drove up to London and parked the bus in Harwood Road.

I was, as they say, seriously shagged after a long squawk. I went in and put on the TV, and I was sitting cross-legged, and must have fallen asleep sitting on my foot. When I woke up it was about 3am and there was white noise on the TV. I got up to turn it off and my whole leg had gone to sleep, and there was nothing there. So when I tried to put weight on it I fell straight down and broke my leg. So there I was at 3am, shagged out, with a fucking broken leg. I couldn't be bothered to do anything about it, so I went to sleep. Next morning the leg had swelled up, and I took it into St Stephens and they patched it up. That was the final irony, that after all the insanity one ends up breaking one's leg watching TV at home. Which was seriously amusing in my view. As they say, if there isn't a God, someone's got an awful lot of explaining to do, and I think he's having a bit of a giggle.

*

We arrived back in England with recriminations over the bus already beginning. Clearly, we had outgrown St Moritz as a venue; we needed to find a resort with a more enlightened attitude to our art form. Eileen suggested Aspen, Colorado; they were approached, and were interested. However, to put on a ski race in the USA, we were going to need over ten times more sponsorship money than we had ever been able to raise before, and we never managed it. Thus the surrealist ski races ended, having provided us, and our billion-plus audience, with a great deal of entertainment. The only people, it seemed, who were not amused, were the dour Swiss.

In his own words: *Martin Berthod*

Kurverein St Moritz, Sportsekretariat
Postfach CH-7500 St Moritz

DSC International Sports Ltd
GB London SW6 7TX
attn. Mr Kirke

<u>Re: Dangerous Sports Club Ski Race</u>
Thank you for your letter about the Classic Ski Race. I understand that you and all the members of the DSC spent a lot of money and time for the races in the last three years. With the three races you brought St Moritz promotion which we probably never had before from a sport event. I agree that there were some things which went wrong in the organization from our part but you can believe me it was really not easy to work with you and your group. If something happened, you never took the responsibility for it...
During our meeting one month before this year's race we decided to organize it on the ski slope down Salastrains because of transport difficulties for the big machines and because the slope on Corviglia was in your opinion not fast and steep enough. I pointed out that this slope was much steeper and more difficult but at the same time you asked to start further up to get more speed...
Not one of this year's machines had a braking mechanism and 90% had no steering facilities. You yourself should be very happy to be still alive after your fall with the motorbicycle. Unfortunately I have to tell you again that you have no ideas about speed and power transmission on a ski slope...
For the last three years we always had problems with your group. I don't want to speak about the expenses of the past two years but also this year we had bills of more than Sw. Fr. 5,000

for damages...
Kind regards,

M Berthod
Manager of sports and events
St Moritz Tourist Office

For a Winter Olympic venue to thank us for bringing them unprecedented promotion was praise indeed, but also frustrating, considering how much more impact the event would have had with the bus. We knew that, for a sum considered modest in most advertising circles, we could stage a magnificent event with not just a bus, but combine harvesters, airliners, and a replica of the Titanic, with iceberg, band and deckchairs. Many ingenious ideas remain for more exciting and rapid smaller machines. There is a whole unexplored field of aerodynamic ski devices, their weight supported by sliding surfaces and their movement controlled by wings and rudders. We may have, 'no idea about power transmission on a slope,' but we remain willing to find out by experiment, unlike our critics, who prefer to stick to the well-proven Høtig method of getting down a hill.

Ed Hulton had once suggested making a square-rigged ice yacht using a DC3 fuselage. It would not be limited to downhill runs, and it might be able to cruise to the North Pole, given a favourable wind. It would be a far more appropriate manner for a gentleman to reach such a destination than the foot-slogging masochism of Sir Ranulph Twisleton-Wykeham Fiennes (Bart), a more traditional kind of upper-class English adventurer who seems to devote his life to tramping around the ends of the earth in the maximum possible discomfort. Why risk losing your toes to frostbite when you could be at the helm of a magnificent ice cruiser, sextant in hand, navigating the frozen wastes in effortless style?

Sadly, the creative staff of advertising agencies can seldom imagine anything more original than a stale re-hashing of whatever worked last time, and remained impervious to our massive ratings. It is easy to assume that any event with such a huge TV audience must be worth a lot of money, but sponsorship eluded us and the 1985 ski race was the end of our experiments in surrealist skiing.

13.

A Tale of Two Beer Companies

'Tie me kangaroo down, sport,
tie me kangaroo down…'
– Rolf Harris

When you see a child holding a bunch of helium-filled balloons, you naturally wonder how many balloons it would take to lift them into the air. (Well, some of us do). Many cartoons have illustrated this concept. When I was about six, I used to read a comic with a science fiction cartoon strip story, in which people ejecting from aircraft floated down under a bunch of balloons, instead of a parachute. A fantasy, or so I thought. Not a bit of it; apparently people have been trying it for years. A man called Arthur Dodds was the first to die in this particular form of aviation, as long ago as 1927, when he flew into a power line.

In his own words: *Hugo Spowers*

I remember one Boxing Day morning, we tried to fly off Beachy Head using balloons. We got some advertising balloons and the idea was to pump them up with helium so that people could leap around thirty feet in the air and jump off Beachy Head, then draw lots, give someone the extra balloons and send him off to France with a few Francs in his pocket.

It was extremely cold, as you can imagine at seven in the morning on Beachy Head, and all the balloons, as we blew them up, were thundering around all over the place and hitting each other. The skin was very brittle in the cold weather and they all burst, so gradually it became quite apparent that it was an impractical plan for the morning's entertainment and we all buggered off.

This experiment in 1981, despite the outcome, was the basis of the suggestion that two people, each supported by a large number of small helium balloons, could hold an aerial duel. They would be launched at the same time, a short distance apart, and would try to shoot each other down using bow and arrow. Each would be able to spare a few balloons to begin with, but before long one of them would be unable to stay up, and could either parachute to the ground, or stay with their balloons and splashdown in water. The first one down would have lost the duel.

Such a competitive Dangerous Sport held little appeal to sponsors. The first real interest we had in anything of this nature was from one of the two Australian beer companies in the British market. The PR company promoting Castlemaine XXXX agreed to fund the construction of a helium-inflatable, kangaroo-shaped balloon, which would not be large enough on its own to lift a person, but would be able to do so if it had four additional ten-foot diameter, round balloons. The overall impression would be of a kangaroo holding a bunch of balloons in its front paws, and carrying a pilot in its pouch.

The round balloons were built by Colt Balloons, whose manager Per Lindstrand went on to partner Richard Branson of Virgin, in a series of ever more expensive ballooning promotions.

The kangaroo itself was built by Gas and Equipment, another company based, like Colt, near Oswestry. Gas and Equipment had a cheery and helpful manager called Craig Marner. Helium is very expensive; each inflation, which would involve the complete loss of the helium, would cost about £1,000, so we couldn't afford the luxury of flight-testing the complete assembly before the real event.

The aim of the kangaroo-balloon project, naturally, was to cross the Channel. We felt very confident that the publicity for this would reach national newspapers, fully justifying the cost. In fact, we offered the client a guarantee on this point. If the crossing failed to get national newspaper coverage, the money paid to the Club would be refunded. We normally offered this guarantee when we approached PR companies, and it was not an empty promise. We knew by this time, that Club activities, big or small, were always considered worth a mention by Fleet Street.

The kangaroo stood fifteen-feet high and was made of a material called urethane. This is the lightest material able to hold helium. The ten-foot diameter supporting balloons were each painted with the XXXX logo. The pilot perched on a seat inside the kangaroo's pouch. The controls were simple; throw out some ballast to go up, and vent some gas, to go down. There was an anchor to throw down on landing.

We set a date to assemble the balloon equipment on Beachy Head and attempt a crossing. Unfortunately the weather was not particularly good, and with the four ten-foot, round balloons inflated, we decided to hold. Mark Chamberlain tied the balloons to a Land Rover, and we went for breakfast.

Shortly afterwards a panic-stricken PR person, Nicky Bright, with the anguished, frightened look of a yuppie who senses that something she is professionally responsible for is about to go dreadfully wrong in public, informed us that one of the balloons had blown loose and flown away. We ran outside, although there was nothing we could do.

'Faaaaaaark!' was all I could think of to say. David managed something slightly more helpful, but there was no pacifying Nicky Bright.

This unfortunate loss put an end to any hope of flying that day, although by that time the weather situation was so obviously unsuitable that the TV company's helicopter had already given up and landed. Without TV coverage the flight would have had no promotional impact.

The PR company were seriously unimpressed by this performance, and we began to argue about paying for a replacement balloon. As usual, we had underpriced the job to the point at which there was no money in reserve to cover disasters like this. Castlemaine's PR company were adamant that they would not pay for a replacement, as the loss was our fault. That may have been true, but their attitude cost them a lot more than the price of one additional small balloon; it cost them the whole promotion. David pulled off a classic dodge; he re-sold the entire project to Fosters Lager.

While the bad vibes were flying, the kangaroo wasn't. It was rotting in the cellar at Shoddy. Urethane has to be stored dry, and Hopalong (we were never very original when it came to naming things) was damp. When we discovered the damage, it was beyond repair, and Hopalong had to be replaced. Craig Marner decided to use PVC for the next one, a more robust material. He also got the job of making a new set of round balloons with the

Fosters brand name on them. Per Lindstrand, still awaiting the final payment for the previous ones, had wisely refused to give us any more credit.

Fosters were delighted with their coup. With the re-sale of the project, there was enough money to pay for an aerial test, and the first flight of the new system took place beside a lake near Bala in Wales, not far from the balloon factory at Oswestry. David Kirke was the pilot. He was launched on what was intended to be a short, shakedown flight at low altitude, giving us experience in assembly and launch of the entire device, and producing pictures and video to use in publicity for the Channel flight. Unfortunately, in a cock-up reminiscent of the Beachy Head fiasco, as he flew over the shore of the lake, David dropped the video camera he was carrying – and as nobody had thought to tie it on, it fell to the water's edge. With the loss of so much weight, the kangaroo rose sharply to over 3,000 ft. As a technician from the local TV company waded knee-deep into the water to retrieve the fallen camera, an expensive professional model, David and Hopalong drifted higher and further away, until they were out of sight.

David then discovered that his gas release valve was stuck, and he was unable to bring the kangaroo down. The higher he flew, the stronger the winds became, and we realised that if he could not get down quickly, he would end up being carried out over the Irish Sea. Finally, after some frantic tugging on the control line, the gas valve came unstuck and he was able to lose altitude. We found him later enjoying some generous hospitality, after landing by a remote house on the coast. David always seemed to have this sort of luck when landing experimental aircraft in random places – it is the luck of the bold.

In August, the ideal time of year to get press coverage for a light-hearted story, we made a second attempt on the Channel crossing. With the gas release valves fixed, we returned to Beachy Head on a day when the wind promised a good chance of making it to France. We set up the kangaroo and tried to launch it, but although it was clearly lighter than air, it refused to rise, as if held down by a giant invisible hand. We realised that the wind was curling over the back of a hillock, creating a downdraft. We guided David and Hopalong up the hill to a better launch site. The kangaroo drifted through a gorse bush as we pulled it along, but fortunately the tough PVC was not holed. Once out of the downdraft, the kangaroo took off and soon became a speck in the blue.

It climbed to over 10,000ft, much higher than intended, and we lost sight of it.

Fosters' PR people were well aware of the misfortunes that had befallen their rivals, and had no wish to share the sad fate of Nicky Bright. For this reason, our agreement with them stated that our payment would only be handed over once the kangaroo actually took off for France. (A successful flight was not a condition of payment, as a traditional British heroic failure would be just as good a story). The moment David was airborne, I took a cheque from the PR company and went straight to the nearest bank.

We then jumped in the VW truck and headed for Dover to retrieve David from France, helping ourselves to the PR company's hospitality supplies as we left, to keep us merry *en route*. Meanwhile, far above us, Captain Andrew Bennett of Air UK, flying from Stanstead to Paris, was reporting the sighting of a kangaroo to a somewhat sceptical air traffic controller.

David flew due East. Any wind direction from East to South would get him to France after travelling about 100km. The wind was just within this allowed range; any further North and he would have ended up with a much longer journey towards Holland, resulting in a ditching. (He wore a waterproof dry-suit as a precaution against having to make a water landing, and carried a two-way radio). After two or three hours, he put down near a village called Ferques (would you believe), which is between Calais and Boulogne. A local farmer kindly obliged by hiding the equipment from the police, in his barn, while we were still on the ferry. David called home to Shoddy, so that Miranda could direct us to the hidden balloons. Then, by making a fast deal with a local reporter, he got a lift to Calais and caught the next boat home.

While David was on the ferry, we found the farmer, and he gave us the equipment and sold us a few bottles of the local *vin ordinaire* as well. When we got back to England, we found that the successful flight had indeed been well-covered in the national press. Fosters were delighted. I am not quite sure what Nicky Bright thought.

Since Hopalong had been spotted and reported, the Civil Aviation Authority felt it had to prosecute David for flying without a pilot's licence. There was a certain amount of legal argument in court over exactly what kind of licence is needed to fly a kangaroo. In the end, it was accepted that it fell into the category of experimental aircraft, as defined by the Air Navigation Order. You are supposed to hold a licence for a related type of conventional aircraft before testing unconventional ones. Also, whatever the aircraft type, you are always supposed to respect the rules of controlled air lanes. David was fined £100. The case brought a fresh round of publicity, even an editorial in *The Times*.

In its own words: *The Times*

…Before everybody concludes that the captain of an airliner has taken his passengers to 10,000ft while in the grip of a massive attack of the DTs, it must be said that he was perfectly sober and in his right mind; there was an enormous kangaroo in his flight path. What is more, there was a man in its pouch.

…The man cadging a lift from the passing beast was the Chairman of the Dangerous Sports Club. Mr Kirke was fined £100 for flying without a pilot's licence. He expressed a due contrition.

There can be few people who already knew, before this business, that it is an offence in this country to fly a kangaroo without first having been licensed to do so; well, they know better now. But what happened to the pilot of the aircraft who had to take prompt evasive action because he had seen a kangaroo bowling merrily through the sky at 10,000ft?

For not only was he sober; he knew he was sober. Yet if he hasn't acquired a permanent cardiac murmur, a facial tic and a tendency to wake screaming from his sleep, airborne kangaroos must be much more common over the Channel than most of us had hitherto supposed.

If he has to take legal action, all those involved should start by blushing at the derisory fine imposed on the man who started the trouble. The law may be an ass, and has frequently made a dog's breakfast; moreover, some judges want to bring back the cat, and others have frequently put the cart before the horse. But it would be a very grave matter indeed if British justice were now to be dispensed in a kangaroo court.

The court case was not concluded until after Hopalong's final flight, however, which involved another launch from Bala Lake for the benefit of photographers, this time from Australia's Channel 9. We drove out on a stunningly beautiful morning, with mist just clearing over the lake. Conditions were perfect for scenic photography. We inflated the kangaroo. This time it was my turn as pilot. Like David, I had never before piloted a balloon, either helium or hot air, but the theory seemed straightforward enough.

I was launched in perfectly still air and rose gently, almost straight upwards. After thirty seconds in the air, the kangaroo began to detach itself from me. This was not as worrying as it might sound, as the only essential parts of the flight system were the round balloons and the pilot's seat. The actual kangaroo was really only decorative. Filled with helium, it was more or less weightless, but did not contribute to the overall lift. Hopalong was simply tied to the pilot, and in fact could be jettisoned if necessary, for example in the event of a water landing. When I realised that Hopalong was slowly falling off me, I caught him and tried to re-make the connections, but once again poor knotting was the curse of the project. (None of us were very good Scouts). In the end I spent most of the flight holding on to him with my left leg.

By alternately releasing gas and pouring away beer, I was trying to maintain a low altitude. It took me some time to adjust to the delay between making a control input and getting some response; if I poured some beer, I would have to wait a couple of minutes before there was a noticeable increase in height. If I released some gas, it would take just as long to respond the other way. Since then, I have flown hot-air balloons, and found that this delay is a characteristic of all lighter-than-air craft, although the length of the delay varies a lot. When you are accustomed to the instant responses of land vehicles, though, it can take a while to get used to the more leisurely art of flying an aircraft which is controlled by pouring beer.

After about twenty minutes Hopalong was becoming harder to hold with my leg, and I needed to land. I vented some gas and came down. When I first touched the ground, Hopalong finally fell off and I went back up. I had been expecting this, and let out enough gas to be able to make long hops by just touching gently down. I was enjoying this, but in the end I was caught and held by the others, who were getting hungry and wanted to get the balloons packed up. We were due to have dinner at the Cafe Royal in London that evening, and we had a long drive ahead. The Australian TV company were hoping to film some childish misbehaviour in high class surroundings that night, and we didn't disappoint them. They were in the process of interviewing Graham over port and cigars when Tommy Leigh-Pemberton was thrown across the table, crashing into Eric's wheelchair (a wheelchair was the easiest way of moving the plaster figure). This drowned the interview with the sound of breaking Waterford crystal and tumbling bottles of Moet. It was exactly what the producer needed to project his image of the English; after all, we think of the Aussies as beer-swilling sheep molesters, so they are entitled to their own misapprehensions about us.

*

After that contribution to international misunderstanding, Hopalong made a few more appearances inflated with air, purely as a static display, but never flew again. Sadly, the cost of helium made it too expensive to fly the kangaroo just for fun. Fosters felt they had got good value for their money and, perhaps wisely, chose to quit while they were ahead.

A few years later, Per Lindstrand and Richard Branson flew a combined gas and hot air balloon across the Atlantic, and subsequently from Japan to Alaska. Although these flights involved considerable technical achievements, I believe they showed that the PR benefits of such things are not proportional to the distance covered. The Japan-Alaska flight did not attract very much press coverage, largely because it coincided with the outbreak of the Gulf War, and Branson returned to more conventional marketing methods.

Special-shaped balloons are very popular today. There are some beautiful flying models of motorcycles, sailing ships, and consumer products. I have even seen a bust of Beethoven drifting across the sky. All of them, of course, are hot-air balloons, which are so much cheaper to fly and easier to handle than gas balloons. Perhaps a flying kangaroo would seem rather tame by today's standards.

A small, basketless type of hot air balloon called a Cloudhopper is commercially available today, in which the pilot, along with his propane supply, dangles directly from the balloon, in a seat-and-harness device very similar to that in our kangaroo. It might be possible to use these for settling matters of honour between gentlemen, although personally, I believe that a system of multiple helium balloons lends itself better than Cloudhoppers, to the original idea of duelling with bows and arrows, which, like so many other interesting ideas, has yet to be tried.

14.

A Sport Becomes a Sausage Machine

'For what do we live, but to make sport for our
neighbours, and to laugh at them in our turn?'
– Jane Austen (*Pride and Prejudice*)

Shortly after the kangaroo adventures, our attention was turned to something altogether more serious, both in itself, and in its implications for our commercial bungee jumping activities. In January 1986, we were hired by the BBC to arrange a bungee stunt for the Saturday evening programme, *Noel Edmonds' Late Late Breakfast Show*. The show was based in a London studio, but featured an outside broadcast (OB) every week, in which an ordinary viewer performed some adventurous activity or stunt. The OB was the climax of the show. Noel Edmonds himself remained in the London studio, while the OB was presented by Mike Smith, who, like Edmonds, was a BBC Radio One disc-jockey turned TV presenter. The show had good ratings (at an important stage of the Saturday night ratings battle), which were widely credited to the popularity of the OB features. Despite this, it appeared that the BBC was reluctant to spend more than the absolute minimum possible on the production. The OB producer, David Nicolson, had to arrange a different production each week, which involved setting up a stunt, rehearsing the volunteer partic-ipant, and finally staging a live outdoor performance; not a small job.

Each stunt was arranged by an expert in the field; if the volun-teer was going to tackle an assault course, for example, an Army PT instructor would supervise them on the day. When they wanted to stage a bungee stunt, the Dangerous Sports Club were the obvious people for the job. We were paid around £1,000 to set up the event, which was only slightly more than the going rate for outdoor shows at the time. For this, Nicolson wanted the services of at least three technically skilled people for two days, plus the use of our bungee equipment. He was getting a bargain. As usual, we were grossly underpriced, but we relied on unpaid members to do the job, and hoped that the exposure would lead to other work.

The stunt itself was a 'bungee catapult', in which the volunteer was to be hurled out of a large Jack in the Box by elastic rope. The location was a dockside in Bristol. In a catapult, the jumper is first tied down to a block of concrete. The crane then goes up to stretch the bungee rope, and the jumper is then cut free and goes flying upwards. On the rehearsal day, a Friday, we set up the bungee ropes for what we considered a comparatively mild catapult. A good, hard catapult sends you scorching upwards, right over the top of the crane, but for the volunteer we thought we would be more gentle. For the sake of thorough testing and setting up camera angles, I made about half a dozen catapult jumps during the day, leaving me stiff-necked.

The next day, Saturday, we did some further tests and a lot of hanging around, something which seems to be an inevitable part of TV work. Over lunch, we had a long chat with David Nicolson about the possibility of doing another job for a later edition of the show, in which a volunteer could make a bungee jump in the normal way, from the top. We told him quite clearly that some of us had been hurt in the past developing this, but that we would use well-proven techniques and could offer a level of safety at least as good as the other stunts featured on the show.

Showtime came round, and at the beginning of the programme, the OB item had a brief introduction. David Kirke lurched in front of the cameras to say hello to Mike Smith and receive the Club's credit for arranging the stunt. In the customary banter between studio and location, Noel Edmonds made the jocular remark, 'He's drunk!', which was not true; since we had responsibility for the safety of the volunteer, we would not drink until after the show. Realising that he could be sued for such comments, Noel later wrote to apologise, and I don't believe any harm was done, except perhaps to relations between us and the BBC.

At the end of the show, the volunteer, a quiet young man who had spent the whole day hanging around, and who probably felt that appearing on TV was not actually so glamorous after all, was duly hurled into the night sky and lowered safely to the dockside. The crowd cheered, and we all breathed a sigh of relief. We went to the pub and thought that was that.

The following November, ten months later, we were as surprised and shocked as anyone else to hear the news that a volunteer participant had been killed in rehearsal for the show, during a bungee jump. There was a public outcry, and the rest of the series was immediately cancelled.

A lot of people pontificated in newspapers, saying that they had always believed it was unwise to get ordinary members of the public to do TV stunts. Some of these commentators were stunt-men who probably felt that they should have had the work themselves. While there is something to be said for this argument, however self-serving, it misses the point, because the appeal of the show rested largely on the fact that an ordinary person was the star. However, the management of the BBC stated that they would never again use a volunteer in a show like this.

As the recognised experts on bungee jumping, our advice was required by the investigating officials. The lawyers acting for the family of the dead man also asked us to find out what had happened, so David and I spent several days looking at the equipment and talking to the people involved. I wrote a detailed report on the technical aspects of the disaster, and submitted it to the coroner. I was shocked at the number of stupid mistakes made in setting up the stunt, and listed them in my report.

The stunt arranger was a joke shop proprietor from Brighton and part-time escapologist, who had no experience of bungee jumping at all. His only qualifications for the job seemed to be that he knew David Nicolson, and that he was prepared to work for even less than us. The equipment they used was badly designed, and none of the critical components had a backup in case of failure. Nobody checked the equipment just before the jump, and nobody was with the volunteer at the time of jumping, to supervise the critical moment. The entire system was untested when the volunteer, a twenty-three-year-old bricklayer, was told to jump. He fell all the way from the top of the crane to the ground, trailing the bungee rope, which had somehow become disconnected from the crane. He was killed on impact.

We may have called ourselves the Dangerous Sports Club, and we had indeed made mistakes and had accidents, but we were never quite so cavalier as this. We never relied on single parts for vital connections, and everybody's equipment, whether for bungee jumping, hang-gliding, balloon flying or whatever, was checked over by someone else immediately before use.

I thought there were three possible causes of the fatal disconnection; firstly, that the stunt arranger had failed to properly connect the top end of the rope to the crane; secondly, that on the way up, the volunteer had unintentionally undone the connection; and third, that the connection had undone itself as the rope paid out. This was possible because they had used a special ice-climbing karabiner, with no screw-lock, as the sole connection between bungee and crane. We found it was so easy to undo, you could open it without even realising, and that if the rope twisted in a certain way, it could undo the link on its own. We shall never know which of the three possibilities was the one which happened, but I think the first is the most likely.

The family were represented at the inquest by James Hunt (no relation to our own Tim Hunt), a barrister with a gravelly voice like Joe Cocker, and devastating questioning technique. Although it was not strictly necessary, David Kirke was determined that the Club should be represented, and our barrister was Ed Fitzgerald. Ed is an old friend of the club and a very sharp barrister who specialises in civil rights cases and often represents people who have suffered miscarriages of justice. The BBC were represented by David Eady QC and his team of juniors. Looking smug, and doubtless overpaid, he attempted vainly to defend the indefensible. The inquest was held at Milton Keynes and lasted five days. All the newspapers sent reporters, keen for scandal and gory detail.

Not long after the disaster, we had been invited by the *Sun* newspaper to perform a bungee jump for them to photograph. I made a couple of jumps for them, in a dreary crane company yard one wet winter day, and the pictures were used in an article about the case, which was strongly critical of the BBC. The coroner therefore asked the jury whether they were *Sun* readers, intending to remove them from the jury if they had seen this article. None of them admitted to being *Sun* readers, a statistically unlikely state of affairs which the coroner ignored.

The inquest began with a description of the victim's injuries, read out by the pathologist who carried out the post mortem. This gruesome recital of the bodily damage caused by high speed ground impact was very upsetting for the family and girlfriend of the victim, and it didn't do much for me either. Various witnesses to the death were called, including the crane driver. By gruesome coincidence, he was also the crane driver at Potterspury when Hugo Spowers broke his legs; the same unfortunate man had been at the controls when the two worst bungee jumping accidents in the short history of the sport had taken place.

The main witnesses were to be David Nicolson, the producer, and Paul Matthews, the stunt arranger. When he first took the stand, Nicolson gave the appearance of not understanding the depth of the trouble he was in. He seemed cocky and self-satisfied, leaning back in his chair and taking the line that the death had been an unlucky accident, like being struck by lightning. He was clearly taken aback to be personally criticised and accused of incompetence. There was an overnight break in his questioning, and on the second day he had quite a different attitude, sitting up and looking almost contrite. The experienced barristers could tell at once that he had been advised on how to give a better impression, although this is against the rules of evidence. However, the change in his manner could not disguise the facts of the case.

As the incompetence of the BBC, the clumsiness of the people it employed, the inadequacy of the way it was managed, and the complete absence of explicit responsibility for safety, were revealed, several things became clear.

Firstly, the BBC had totally ignored the Health and Safety at Work Act, and it would be prosecuted for this. Secondly, they would have to pay the family of the victim a substantial amount in compensation. Thirdly, it was a possibility that the jury would bring in a verdict of unlawful killing – which would mean someone would be charged with manslaughter, probably Nicolson. Fourthly, the heavy press coverage of the death would spoil the market for bungee jumping in the UK, even as a display event, let alone as a mass participation sport, for some years. With one or two exceptions, nobody in Britain was willing to hire out cranes to bungee jumpers for years afterwards.

After the day in court, the lawyers would meet each other and negotiate. If the verdict was unlawful killing, the BBC would be in a great deal of trouble, literally being accused of killing someone in the name of light entertainment. The actual individuals charged could face prison. However, if the verdict was accidental death (or death by misadventure, which is much the same), the BBC would only face the Health and Safety charge, a comparatively small thing. In that case, the question of compensation for the family would be settled by a civil suit for damages. Since the victim was single, his family would not get very much; in British law, the value of the damages would be based on the victim's potential earnings, which would mean a relatively small sum compared to, for example, libel damages.

The BBC was very much on the defensive at the inquest. They were under pressure from the family's lawyers to agree a sum of compensation out of court, before the inquest verdict. The night before the end of the inquest, the BBC gave in to this pressure and agreed to settle by paying a sum which was much higher than a court would have awarded for damages. Various amounts in the area of £200,000 were reported in the press, but they were guessing, and the actual amount was kept confidential by us, the BBC, and the victim's family.

On the last day, a few tail-end witnesses were called. David Kirke and myself appeared as expert witnesses to comment on technical matters, but we knew that the horse-trading over the money had been done the night before, and there was actually little left for us to say that had not already emerged. The coroner's questions (on technical matters) to earlier witnesses had largely followed the line of my written report, and so the essential points had already been made. David Eady, the BBC's QC, asked me some curious questions about a bungee show some years previously, trying to make me admit that I had allowed unsafe jumping (which I hadn't). I stonewalled and he gave up. It wasn't worth his while trying any harder to discredit me, given that it would not change anything. I thought it was a low tactic for him to try, but that's how most lawyers operate.

The coroner summed up the evidence at great length, and sent the jury out. They came back after a couple of hours to ask for some legal advice. Could they add a rider to their verdict, saying that they thought the BBC had failed in its legal duty of care? Clearly, they believed that the law had been broken, but that a verdict of unlawful killing was too strong – perhaps sounding too much like deliberate murder. A verdict of misadventure, though, would appear to let those responsible off the hook. The traditional choice of verdicts offers nothing in between these extremes, and they wanted to invent a new verdict somewhere in the middle.

The coroner made it clear that he would prefer them to stick to the traditional choice of verdicts. Another hour passed, and they returned with a verdict of death by misadventure.

Although nobody faced manslaughter charges over the incident, the BBC were fined £2,000 for breaking the Health and Safety at Work Act, and there was some internal re-organisation concerning responsibility for safety within the BBC. However, the reputation of bungee jumping within the UK sank to an all-time low, and it took years to recover. During this period, companies in Australia, New Zealand, America, France and elsewhere sprang up, offering bungee jumps from cranes and bridges, to the public. Some of those countries have relatively slack laws on public safety, and these companies were able to establish a considerable commercial base, despite a number of accidents and even some fatalities.

Back in 1984, a man called John Priest had written to me from New Zealand asking for technical information on bungee jumping. I wrote back describing our experiences. A few months later he sent me a picture of a bridge and a letter raving about the fun he'd had jumping it. He did not, it seemed, intend to pursue bungee jumping any further at that time. If that was the first bungee jump in New Zealand, though, it certainly wasn't the last. In 1988, a man called A J Hackett, who was inspired by seeing film of the Club's jumps from the Golden Gate bridge, set up a commercial jumping business at a bridge near Queenstown in New Zealand. Queenstown is a big resort, and the large number of gung-ho young tourists with money to spend gave him a ready market, which, along with the low overheads, made the venture a success. Another commercial venture began in America, run by John Kockelman.

Similar companies spread rapidly, setting up crane-based sites all over New Zealand and Australia. They used home-made bungee rope, without the braided outer cover of our shock cord, and ankle 'harnesses' which were simply a towel around the ankles and a strap tightened around the towel. Despite the BBC tragedy, many of them were still using single karabiners in vital connections (and many still do). Inevitably, fatal accidents did happen. One company managed to drop Miss Australia off Sydney Harbour Bridge without a secure harness, and she fell from the fully-stretched rope into the water. Remarkably, she was not seriously hurt, but they were lucky not to have a dead beauty queen on their hands. As a result of such disasters, bungee jumping was banned for a couple of years in France and in parts of

Australia. After some time, though, it was accepted once again, and it is now carried on commercially all over the world. Most of the companies involved operate like sausage factories, processing jumpers as fast as possible and viewing them only as economic units.

A J Hackett's company spread to France in 1990, following his publicity stunt of a jump from the Eiffel Tower. By this time, they faced some well-established local competition from French companies. By 1991, bungee jumping had reached the point at which it was acceptable once again in the UK. Several companies wanted to set up in business. Ten years on from the pioneering days, I had more or less lost interest in it, and I didn't want to earn a living in a sausage machine operation. There was still some amateur jumping going on in the UK, the most regular jumpers being ex-Club member David Aitkenhead, and a new student group called the Oxford Stunt Factory. The Stunt Factory was run by Ding Boston, who had been on the fringes of the Club for many years.

Since fully commercial bungee jumping was inevitably going to spread to the UK, what was needed was a set of ground rules to provide companies with a legal basis to operate, to maintain safety standards, and ensure a fair market.

Ding suggested we should start an organisation called BERSA, the British Elastic Rope Sports Association, which would become the governing body of bungee jumping in the UK. We wrote a Code of Safe Practice for bungee jumping operators. The Code became the safety handbook for commercial operators in the UK, the home country of bungee jumping. Several companies started up, including some run by French- and New Zealand-trained people, alongside those in the British tradition. They have now been safely run for several years.

So, the wheel has turned once more; in little over a decade, a brand new sport had been pioneered in Britain by a group of individualists, turned into an industry by foreigners, and now it has its own regulatory bodies, books of rules, and professional instructors. It all happened so fast. It is often said that the British can innovate but fail to exploit. I believe it, as I have seen it happen with bungee jumping. Chris Baker's idea, pioneered in Bristol, was first commercialised on the other side of the world, so successfully that many people actually believe that bungee jumping was invented in New Zealand. Our failure to beat them to it was only partly the result of unfortunate circumstance; even without the BBC disaster to hold us back, we didn't have the commercial vision to market the idea and establish an industry the way others did, in particular A J Hackett. Actually, we never really tried, since establishing industries was not our purpose.

*

Many areas of elastic rope sport remain which are not yet fully explored. For years, I wanted to experiment with elastic water-ski towing line, but I have never been able to try it properly, as my canal houseboat is a bit too slow for water skiing. Catapulting is not widely practised commercially because of the slow turn-around time, so is a little-known field. Also, I have always wanted to experiment with a variation of ski-jumping using bungee rope catapults to fling people into the air without the usual giant ramp. It could make big jumps possible almost anywhere.

Another variation is called horizontal bungee jumping, or bungee running. A kind of bungee running was used in the early 1970's game show *Jeux Sans Frontieres*, in which a competitor, pulling against elastic rope, was sprayed with fire hoses by the opposition. Nowadays, this sort of thing is often practised in the garden of a pub; the bungee is fixed to a wall, and the runner has to get as far as they can, pulling against the rope. Normally a glass of beer is placed as a target for them to reach. The common result is that they end up slipping and being dragged backwards, tearing clothes and skin alike, to the amusement of onlookers. The dangers of bungee running were recently highlighted in the British Medical Journal, which described the case of a runner who got to maximum stretch, then heard a loud snap as the rope pulled free of the wall. He waited for a terrible second, heard an ominous whistling sound, and was hit in the left buttock by the full force of the rope. This created a lesion so severe it had to be surgically drained. Had it hit him a few inches to the right, I thought, the rope could have disappeared altogether.

15.

A Flash in Japan

'I don't think we're in Kansas any more, Toto.'
– Dorothy (*The Wizard of Oz*)

The Club continued to scratch a living through the middle-Eighties, earning modest fees for work which most of us found quite amusing, if not always thrilling. In May 1986, we were visited by two rather peculiar people from Japan. They were known as the Kawa-Sans and they were a strange couple, even by Japanese standards of weirdness; they stood alongside karaoke and bonsai trees as Oriental peculiarities.

The Kawa-Sans were taking part in a TV show with the meaningless title *Kan Kan Gaku Gaku*. From what we could gather, it was like the notorious 'torture show' called *Endurance*, in which contestants are physically and mentally abused until they can bear it no longer. I do not believe the Kawa-Sans were competing for cash like the contestants on *Endurance*, but, for some inscrutable reason, they had been selected to suffer at our hands to entertain their compatriots. We were invited to maltreat them in our own peculiar ways during their three day visit to the UK.

The invitation came from a Japanese TV director based in London whose name was Aki. I got to know Aki in 1984, when he had filmed me performing a bungee jump. Aki was Japanese himself, but had not fitted into the straightjacket of Japanese life, choosing to live in the West instead. He made a living supplying film of British life to Tokyo Broadcasting Systems, the Japanese equivalent of the BBC. Our relationship with Aki continued for some years, often uneasily. We were exactly what he wanted in some respects; we were distinctly English, eccentric, and could provide visual entertainment which would confirm all the myths the Japanese have about Britain (they have as many about us as we have about them). On the other hand, we could be difficult to deal with. Aki, being a bit of a square peg himself, could understand us, but his producer, Shuji Homma, never quite worked out what made us tick.

We fetched the Kawa-Sans from Heathrow using Xan's double-decker bus, which he had kept after the great disappointment at St Moritz and which we used for parties, going to rock festivals, and so on. We took them to the studio in Boundary Row where Steve Smithwick worked. Steve was a scenery and props constructor, and specialised in making highly realistic severed limbs for horror movies. His studio was littered with heads, arms and mutilated bodies, scattered among half-painted theatrical scenery as if by some nocturnal axeman. It all made a suitable backdrop for breakfast. We had ordered a large take-away from the Kabana Tandoori, and Mahendra had prepared his fire-hot curry for us, which was obtainable at the Kabana by special request only. The Kawa-Sans were seated in the middle of a long table. At the head was Steve, the host, who at that particular, post-punk moment, may well have been the only man in Europe with green hair and purple boots (his appearance usually depended on his latest job). Around the table were about fifteen hungry Club members, some more dishevelled than others, but none averse to a good hot curry except for the priapic plaster man Eric, who did not count eating curry among his vices, and who sat quietly smoking.

The Kawa-Sans were not accustomed to food that hurts, which was a common form of masochism among the Club, but apparently not among the Japanese. Soon the sweat was pouring down their faces. I was having some difficulty myself, and I had the advantages of considerable practice and a glass of water. David particularly relished their suffering; something about foreigners brought out his sadistic side. I think he saw the whole exercise as a means of exacting symbolic revenge on the Japanese for Britain's humiliation over the fall of Singapore.

By this time it had become clear that the Kawa-Sans could be divided into a leader and a follower, who we called Manual and Automatic. Manual was in the habit of making odd gestures and uttering raucous, ritualistic cries, while the silent Automatic generally sat cross-legged looking up at him, or followed him around on hands and knees. Both wore black tunics and trousers, which is standard school uniform in Japan, although they were clearly past school age.

When Manual finally managed to swallow a lump of meat, he retreated from the table and cried, 'Banzai!'. I had thought that this Japanese battle cry was perhaps a myth I had picked up from comics and war movies, but Manual exclaimed it quite often. When they had eaten all they could manage, they were finally permitted a drink of water. Manual, who spoke a little English, stood up and made a toast to us, saying 'My blood to you,' (he pronounced it 'brud') and flicked drops of water around the table.

Following the sado-masochistic breakfast, our guests were flown to Scotland for a visit to a distillery. Scotch whisky is one of our biggest exports to Japan, and the whisky companies are always keen to get publicity there, so had no qualms about letting the cameras in. The Kawa-Sans were put to work cleaning out a mash tun, a job which involves swimming in a morass of warm, overwhelmingly smelly barley mash, which resembles the primordial soup and would probably give rise spontaneously to new life if not regularly cleaned out. Our own champion mash diver, Willy Purcell, jumped in to show them the way. He managed this without revealing that his left leg was artificial; he had lost the original due to electrocution while riding on top of a train in Switzerland. Later, he was able to play one of his favourite nasty tricks on Manual. He invited Manual to stamp on his (artificial) foot as hard as possible, in a game like 'slaps' or 'knuckles'. Willy – who was fluent in Japanese – gave a terrible cry and feigned agony. When he had 'recovered', it was his turn to stamp on Manual's foot. This time there was no faking the pain.

The next day we took them out to Loch Ness, to be used as monster-bait. Our fishing craft included Nellie, and Wally Blacker's Red Baron aeroplane, mounted on floats. This event was simply an excuse for some scenic shots and a short talk about the monster, but did allow the unfortunate victims to be immersed in the coldest water I have ever come across in liquid form. While launching the various craft, I had to put a foot into the Loch occasionally, and each time, my leg instantly went numb with cold.

The last day of their ordeal was back in England, bungee jumping and catapulting with a crane. Both were subjected to what they obviously found a terrifying experience, and Aki was delighted with the result. This was just what Japanese TV audiences wanted to see. Manual and Automatic were finally allowed to go home.

This show must have been well received, because it led to an invitation for us to go to Japan to do some bungee jumps. Three of us were asked to appear on a programme whose name was roughly translated as *Super People of the World*. This is an annual, two-hour show produced by NTV of Japan, which had high audience ratings, in which various foreigners who are somehow unusual or interesting are displayed like beasts in a human zoo.

David Kirke, Mark Chamberlain and myself went to Japan to make this appearance. On arrival, we were driven to a hotel near Mount Fuji, where we were accommodated along with Aki and Shuji Homma. David was constantly suspicious of Aki, and often accused him of taking an excessive commission for setting up the appearance, which caused Aki some indignation, and Mark and I some embarrassment. We tended to keep apart when not busy filming.

Like all TV work, there was a great deal of waiting involved. When the crane arrived, we found that the Japanese had built a personnel carrier for the jump which was remarkably well suited to the purpose. It was sturdy, had a hole in the floor for the bungee rope to pass through, and another hole beside that, for filming. The gate area was uncluttered and easy to jump from, and all in all, it was a pleasure to work in. Similar designs are now used around the world at commercial bungee jumping centres, and I have since dispatched many first-timers from them. It was a big improvement over the clumsy old cages and cement buckets we were used to before then.

We made a number of jumps, and David was filmed from several angles jumping from the top and catapulting from the bottom. The weather was wet, but the film satisfied the director, and the next day we went back into Tokyo.

The air was warm, humid and dirty in Tokyo, and many people walked around wearing what looked like surgeons' face masks. We found our way around during the day, visiting the Tokyo Tower, a second-rate copy of the Eiffel Tower (disappointingly, not jumpable), and Akihabara, a vast shopping area, crowded with hundreds of shops selling the latest electronic devices. At night, we went out in Roppongi, a lively and cosmopolitan area, popular with expatriates. We also had one sad appointment to keep. By an awful coincidence, our old friend Willy Purcell had died in Tokyo a week earlier when he fell out of a window. We had hoped to meet him and get up to some mischief together, but instead we had to go to his funeral.

We were accommodated in the Capital Tokyu Hotel, one of the city's five-star hotels whose normal guests are government officials and representatives of large companies with big expense accounts. The entire top floor was occupied by Michael Jackson, who was starting a worldwide concert tour in Tokyo that week. The performers on the NTV show were housed on the fifth floor. They were a bewildering bunch. They fell into three categories; performing artists with an unusual act; physical freaks; and various others who were simply strange or peculiar. I put ourselves in the first category, along with a group of Chinese acrobats, various jugglers, and a trick cyclist.

The physical freaks included two pairs of twins so identical that their husbands could not tell them apart, an American woman with unusually long arms, an Australian man so thin that he had won the title 'Mr Puny-verse', two extremely tall men and a dwarf, a hugely obese man who was described as the heaviest person in the world, and two American women who had abnormally swollen mammary glands. This was getting fairly tacky, but the third category took the biscuit.

The just-plain-weird group included a double-jointed man who could play the guitar behind his back (unfortunately he only knew Country & Western songs); a man who would spend hours balanced on two legs of a chair, while perched on the edge of a tall building; and the married couple with the greatest age difference in the world. The wife was almost senile and could only just walk, and the husband was a young man in his twenties. We thought this was about the most tasteless item in a fair collection. I wondered whether the Japanese could actually see any difference between people who did something novel or unusual, people who were born with a physical peculiarity, and people who were just, plain, four-hundred-toothbrushes-in-the-cuckoo-clock barking mad. We hardly felt that, for example, the Chinese acrobats, who were brilliantly skilled performers and could reasonably be described as Super People, really belonged on the same show as the giants, dwarfs, huge breasts or double-jointed guitarist.

For me, though, the strangest contrast of all was that this menagerie of freaks, weirdos and crazies, were sharing a hotel with Michael Jackson, who was then being paid millions of dollars to try to make people actually care about the alleged difference between Pepsi and Coke. To my mind, that was far more crazy and surreal than anything or anyone on our floor. If I ever needed an answer to those seat-belt-and-safety-net enthusiasts who thought BASE jumping was perverse, I would point to the values of a world in which a company selling tooth-rotting, artery-clogging syrup, is worth enough money to provide clean water, adequate food and basic education to all those who lack them. Now there's perverse for you.

The recording went on in two evening sessions. Our item was in the first session. David was brought into the studio to meet the presenter, the film of the bungee jumping was shown, and there was a slow and rather dull interview through a translator. Also in this session were the acrobats, who had an unbelievable balancing display, and a contortionist who performed incredible feats of flexibility and physical control, all while balancing five trays of glassware. I was watching very closely, but even at the time I could not work out how she did it. I never knew the human body could bend in those directions. Then the various tall, short and fat people came on and were measured, painfully slowly, and Mr Punyverse was brought in, to display his meagre frame and be suitably ridiculed.

Actually Mr Punyverse was a very down-to-earth Australian, complete with an Australian's appetite for beer. We got on very well, and that evening Mark and I had a session with him. It was hot indoors, and David was having another argument with Aki, so after the bar closed, the three of us went up the fire escape and on to the roof of the hotel to look out over the city. (Mark and I, as BASE jumpers, tended to explore the roof of any building more than ten floors high out of habit). Eventually our whisky bottle was empty, and we looked around for a way down.

The hotel had fixed the main lifts so that they wouldn't stop at Michael Jackson's floor, in an attempt to keep out fans and reporters. However, on the roof there was a service building containing the heating and air conditioning equipment, and a door to the service lift. We decided to try it, and found that it was able to stop on Jackson's floor. Unable to resist, we thought we should check it out. Stepping out of the lift, we found ourselves in a corridor, which was entirely wrapped in polythene sheeting and which had a red carpet laid along the floor. Most of the rooms in the corridor were sealed off, the doors covered by plastic sheet. We crept along to the central area where the main lifts were. The Presidential Suite was off to one side, occupying one third of that floor of the hotel. Quietly we crept into the entrance lobby of the suite, where a Japanese man was asleep at a desk.

We had heard all the rumours about Michael Jackson being strange, and sleeping in an oxygen tent with his pet monkey. The plastic sheeting and new carpet confirmed this for us. 'Hey, you guys, he really is wacko, he should be on our floor!' said Mr Punyverse. We crept towards the suite to have a look. The room was completely dark. I whispered, 'Well, what are we going to do if we find him, set fire to his hair or something?' However, this debate got no further, as the guard stirred in his sleep. We retreated to the main lifts. These could stop at Jackson's floor only if summoned from that level. The lift door opened, and the guard suddenly woke up with a start, jumped over his table, and ran towards us. We pressed the down button, and the lift door closed on him in the nick of time, cutting off a flow of Japanese which, although we didn't speak the language, we understood only too well.

The next evening the TV recording was completed. Out came the grotesque married couple, who were interviewed, and were then made to dance to romantic music and kiss in close-up. The old woman looked very confused. The C&W guitarist dislocated his arms one more time and played his song. The two women with enormous tits came on, took off their bras and were measured by the presenter. They were then invited to place their vast glands on scales; for some reason, it seemed important to record their exact size and weight, as if this made the ten-minute ogle somehow less tacky.

*

On the way back, we paused briefly in Moscow airport. The plane was refuelled, and took on new meals. When I got back to my houseboat, I spent the night in the most intense pain I had ever known. My innards were tying themselves in knots and I was paralysed with agony. It had to be a vengeful God punishing me for some especially outrageous sin; I wondered which. This was gut-rot as I had never known it before; force-eight on the intestinal Richter scale.

Next morning, when I was able to walk again, I went, exhausted, to a doctor. He diagnosed gastro-enteritis, and cheerfully told me that airline meals are a common cause of this complaint; no doubt the chicken I had eaten on the last leg of the flight, prepared in Moscow, was contaminated. I was almost disappointed; it had not been an angry, Old Testament-type God after all, merely a vengeful chicken. Another event with a twist in the tail for me. Altogether it had been a strange trip.

16.

An Arrangement for Strings and Sledgehammers

'Art is not a mirror, it is a hammer.'
-Henry Cow

As well as putting on performances for TV and staging events like ski races and expeditions, the Club had several other projects lurching forwards, backwards, or more often round in circles. One of them was our Big Movie. Graham Chapman, who had joined the Club to go on the Ecuador expedition, had some experience of writing movies. With his Monty Python partners, he had been involved in writing and producing movies like *Life of Brian* (in which he played Brian), *The Meaning of Life*, and also various other movies outside the Python *ouvre*. He had good contacts in the Californian movie industry.

The prospect of making a Hollywood movie was an enticing one which had been on the agenda ever since the relative success of the short film, *The History of the Dangerous Sports Club*. Graham was just the person to advance this project. However, *History…* had been a documentary, originally planned as a TV production. It was cheaply made compared to a feature film, and was released to cinemas as a supporting B-movie, not the main attraction. Nobody shows supporting films any more, and we could not hope to repeat the short, documentary formula for a full-length main feature. That format might work on TV, but to put bums on seats in cinemas, we needed star actors and a fictional storyline. Our first move was to write a treatment.

A treatment is a written explanation of an idea for a movie. It may be just a few short pages, or it may come close to being a full script. When you have written a treatment, you take it to production companies, looking for a development deal. This deal involves the production company paying you money, sometimes tens of thousands of dollars, to go away and write a complete script, do location research, invent budgets, schedules, and other lies, and basically come up with a project which is ready to go into actual production. At this point the developed idea will probably be shelved until the production company feels the market is right for such a film and the appropriate actors are available. The large majority of developed ideas never go into production, but a development deal is still worth having for its own sake. Needless to say, the tricky bit is approaching the production company and getting the deal. It helps to have a recognised name and some contacts.

Graham, David Kirke and I sat down to write a treatment. We used to meet at Graham's house in Kent, usually on Mondays. We would spend most of the day discussing ideas, then I would go home and type out what we had come up with, and send a print-out to the other two. We would use this as a basis for the next session. We came up with a cast of fictitious characters, loosely based on real Club members, or combinations of the characteristics of real members. The starting point of the plot was the hang-gliding expedition to Ecuador. As Graham's first Club activity, it seemed a reasonable place to begin. The story would follow a new member joining the Club, and going on an expedition to the Andes. This character, who was quite sympathetic at the outset, would be easy for the audience to identify with. Later in the plot it would emerge that he had joined the Club with ulterior motives, and was using the expedition as a cover to spy for a giant company which made huge profits exploiting tribal land in the South American rain forest. Although originally working for the bad guys, the hero would turn out to be good at heart in the end. The rain forest stuff was a new concern to the wider world at the time and has since become hackneyed, of course, but at the time, we thought it had something over the usual, banal action-movie plots, which all seemed to feature either Russians or drug dealers as baddies.

The purpose of the storyline was to make the movie something more than a long collection of action sequences, although naturally the movie was intended to be strong on stunts of a fairly surreal nature. Over the course of many meetings, we improved the plot and enlarged the treatment until it was about forty pages long. Whenever I looked at it as a whole, the plot usually seemed to me to be contrived and awkward, but that's how most movie plots are. I suggested providing a physical object as a centre of attention, what Alfred Hitchcock used to call a 'McGuffin', and came up with a computer containing important mineral survey results. This would be the 'football' that would change hands several times in the story, and provide a focus for competition between the goodies and the baddies. Graham liked the idea and it became part of the story. Being a nuts-and-bolts man, I was most concerned with plot mechanics and with making the story consistent. David was more concerned with themes and characters, while Graham was the one best able to see the movie in his mind's eye. Despite our different backgrounds (Graham was a doctor before turning to comedy), we actually worked together very much like scientists, testing and rejecting many ideas. I found it fascinating.

A time came when we had written enough to present the treatment to production companies. On his next trip to California, Graham took the treatment with him, and showed it to various contacts. On the whole, the reaction was positive, but no development deal was offered. When Graham came back, we had more meetings and made some changes, and he tried again later. Once again, people showed polite interest, but not quite enough. Despite our initial high hopes of an urgent call from Steven Spielberg, it became clear that we were not going to get the deal we had hoped for. After Graham's second trip I personally felt that our chances of getting development money were very low, but David remained optimistic, and Graham still felt the project had potential. In the end, the treatment was instrumental in raising some money, but not in the way we originally wanted.

In 1987, David, and an accountant called Red Donnelly, put together a plan to raise some capital under the Business Expansion Scheme. This was a way of raising money from rich people, who got income tax concessions on the money they invested. The proposed BES was for the Dangerous Sports Club Film Company Ltd, and we rather optimistically hoped to raise £60,000 - £70,000. The film company was assigned the rights to all the film the Club had at that time, and the rights to the movie treatment. This made it a classic speculative investment. If the treatment could attract a development deal, and possibly even go into production, these rights would be worth a lot. Otherwise there would be no return at all. As investments go, it was like an oil well or a gold mine. Either you strike it rich or you lose all your money.

We attracted about £20,000 from eight individuals, less than we'd asked for, and it didn't last long, much of it just paying off existing debts. In the end, of course, we never got a development deal and the company never made any money, and was dissolved in 1991 by the Company Registrar, because it failed to make annual returns.

It was not the first time that some part of the business had been put up for sale. Since the mid-Eighties we had been looking for an overall sponsor, who would pay enough to meet our routine over-head costs, and in return would have their brand name attached to everything we did. Sadly, we never reached this happy state, perhaps because the word 'Dangerous' frightened off the adver-tising people. Sometimes companies were willing to sponsor an individual event, and those which did were always well rewarded in publicity terms, but that was as far as we got.

In 1985, David called a meeting of the seven leading Club members, and proposed that we should each put up £2,000 a year. This would meet most of the basic overhead costs, and provide a certain level of security from which we could mount events and seek further sponsorship. In return, the seven would be rewarded with a dividend if the Club made a profit, but if it didn't, we would each have lost an affordable amount. This suggestion went down like a lead balloon. All of us knew by then that a business run by David was most unlikely to make a profit, as he was temperamen-tally incapable of cost control. Besides, David had chosen to make the Club his business venture, and in doing so he had assumed the usual risks of being a small businessman. The rest of us had chosen other paths in life and did not care to act as his cash cows. We contributed man-hours rather than money. A basic weakness in the Club was the conflict between the ideals of a traditional, amateur group, and the fact that this Club was a small business owned and run by one man, hoping, if not managing, to make a profit. David went to great lengths to maintain the atmosphere of the original, amateur Club days, succeeding to the extent that many people contributed their efforts in the spirit of fun, without feeling that they were just unpaid workers for someone else's company. However, we all drew the line at outright cash subsidy.

Graham continued to put forward the treatment to film producers, and often got expressions of interest which raised hopes of a development deal. In the end, though, the project ended in the most tragic way possible. Graham developed cancer, and in 1989, after a long struggle against the disease, he died. Graham was a reformed alcoholic who had adopted an almost excessively healthy diet, but his one remaining habit was his pipe, and he succumbed in the end to a type of cancer linked to pipe smoking.

I last visited him in hospital about three days before he died. He was in a cheerful, forward-looking mood, and talked at some length about his plans for the future. As a qualified doctor he must have known he was about to die, but he stubbornly refused to take a ringside seat even in the last days of his life, preferring to look ahead to new performances on stages he would not live to tread. He was very enthusiastic when I told him I had just been short-listed to become an astronaut. He was very confident that I would be selected to fly in space. He was cheerful and positive to the last. It upset him when, soon after he began his cancer treatment, the *Sun* printed a story saying that he had AIDS. He complained that they were stereotyping him because he was openly gay. By way of apology, he was given a page in the *Sun* to write an encouraging article about modern cancer treatment, a typically positive thing for him to do.

After years of tempting fate, taking chances and risking our necks, death had finally taken one of us, not by some crash, fall or impact, but by natural causes. Graham's death upset everyone who knew him, and David in particular was profoundly depressed by it. Submerged in our grief was the knowledge that any remaining, slim chances for our Hollywood film project had died with Graham.

The Business Expansion Scheme did not raise enough money to buy a property, which was one of our long term goals. In 1986, the Club office had moved out of Shoddy and we were based in one end of Steve Smithwick's studio in Boundary Row, near Waterloo. Although it was in many respects a good place to be, it was only a temporary situation. David felt that we ought to have our own place, somewhere suitable for our office requirements and equipment storage. To be honest, though, there was also a feeling that, in London in the mid-eighties, a lot of people seemed to be making money out of property, and those who weren't on the bandwagon were somehow missing out. With hindsight, of course, it would have been a disastrous mistake to buy at the peak of the property market. The desire to follow the crowd in this way should have rung alarm bells for a group whose main strength lay in running in the opposite direction to the herd. Only in jest did we recognise that the urge to buy was a symptom of our decline.

We found an old building in Munton Road, near Waterloo. It was a small warehouse with space for storage and offices, and it had a courtyard enclosed by a wall and a pair of sturdy gates. It was derelict inside, and would need completely refitting, starting with plumbing and wiring. David made an offer for it, which was accepted, and pending the exchange of contracts we began working on it. We made a plan and decided the first thing to do was to demolish the existing partitions and start the interior work from scratch.

The obvious way to do this was to hold a sledgehammer party. We arranged one in January of 1987, with a string quartet, a dance band and sledgehammers all round. The singer of the dance band was my close friend Dan Gold, and we decided that when the band finished playing, we would get ourselves up in drag and attending the party as femmes fatales.

The party was a big success, and one of the best attended the Club ever held. Dan's band played a short set, while some of the party-goers explored the roof of the building. The warehouse next door belonged to a wine business, and was fitted with a burglar alarm system on the roof, which the climbers set off. This led to the first visit to the party by the police that night. When they came in they were a little surprised to see people diving through partitions and smashing walls with sledgehammers while others stood around eating peanuts, but once the alarm was turned off, they left. As soon as they were out of sight Dan and I left quietly to get changed.

Forty minutes later we returned, looking like a couple of tarts straight out of a *fin de siècle* Parisian brothel. I had a blonde wig and Dan had a dark one. We had both shaved clean to the bone and Nina Knox-Peebles, David's current Girl Friday, had made us up so that nobody recognised us, not even a few, intimate friends who we thought should know us well enough to see through any disguise. Upstairs the string quartet were playing, accompanied by the crashing sound of sledgehammer on wall below. Confidently we approached David, hoping to fool him, but after picking our way through the rubble, we had quite forgotten to walk like ladies, and we probably moved more like a couple of Welsh fly-halves than seductive bimbos, and he saw straight through our disguise. (Since then I have practiced feminine deportment and made great improvements).

As the party went on, plaster dust mingled with smoke and music to create a haze of sound and light. Out of the haze would come the 'butler' we had hired, a man called Beaumont, who moved around the party making empty glasses disappear and producing clean ones as if by magic, and who carried several bottles of wine which also came and went by sleight of hand. Weaving through the wreckage and dodging the swinging hammers, he kept the wine flowing until, by midnight, the interior walls had all been smashed to pieces, and the string quartet were packing up to leave. Their leader came to David for payment, and from the look in his eyes when David gave him a company cheque, I could tell he knew it would bounce. The police came round again, following a noise complaint, and they were obviously getting irritated. At the time, a whole new industry was starting up which involved holding unauthorised parties in warehouses, and the police had their hands full with such events.

Eventually we were left with a pile of rubble and empty bottles. Naturally, we put off the clearing up until later. As soon as I left the building I was confronted by three policemen who were obviously lurking in the area waiting for people leaving the party. One of them was a trainee on his first night out, and in between questions to me, the senior constable would turn to the trainee and explain the finer points of making an arrest. On the flimsiest of excuses (i.e. I was drunk), I was asked to accompany them to Southwark police station. I was still dressed like a French tart, and was subjected to the full brunt of Metropolitan police sarcasm. At this time of night all they normally have for company are addicts and car thieves, so I suppose a tipsy transvestite wielding a sledgehammer provided them with some light entertainment. I was searched for drugs (with much amusement over my bra stuffing), and as I had my car keys on me, I was tested on a breath analysis machine. I was found to be just under the limit (to my great surprise), and they let me go.

*

After the party, no further progress was made towards buying and renovating the building in Munton Road. On February 19th we had a board meeting of DSC International Sports, which was the company trying to buy the building. We were supposed to exchange contracts the next day, but we were just a trifling amount short of the necessary sum of money to proceed with this. About £74,000 short, in fact. We had tried to get a commercial mortgage, but an inflatable pink elephant might as well pass through the eye of a needle; the company had no regular, reliable income, as well as a history of overdrafts as long as a bungee rope at full stretch, and no-one in their right mind was going to lend the Club money. The deal fell through, and not much later Cosmo Hulton bought the building for re-development. I hope he liked the alterations.

It was our barge-pole financial status, rather than the wisdom to follow our contrary, against-the-tide instincts, which saved the Club from getting burned in the property collapse which came not long after. It is hard to defy conventional wisdom all the time, and hardest of all when the bandwagon has reached full tilt and almost everyone else is aboard. It was a test we failed, and there would be others.

17.

Brake Fluid and Giant Balls

'I often wonder what the vintners buy, one half
so precious as the goods they sell.'
– Omar Khayyam

If people interrupted their useful, productive lives to ask me, 'Are you a member of the Dangerous Sports Club?', or, 'How do you become a member?', I tried to explain that the Club was a chaotic pool into which some plunged head first, while others dipped a toe occasionally, and that nobody was really a member in any formal sense. This was not because we feared limiting a delicate art form by defining it too rigidly. We simply felt that the time and money that might go into producing such absurdly spurious paperwork as membership cards would be better spent on something more exciting (or, failing that, in the bar), and I think we were right.

However, desperation being the mother of the ridiculous, the need to generate steady income eventually led us to set up a formal membership scheme, in which people who cared to pay £50 would be issued with a card, put on the *Nurdorandum* mailing list, and given the opportunity to join in all Club activities. We hoped the scheme would bring new blood, as well as cash, into the Club, although I was sceptical of this. In the end, we did recruit a few good, new people to the Club after this scheme began in 1986, but some of them would probably have joined anyway.

The scheme had an additional, higher tier, called Committee Membership, for which people paid £200 a year. They supposedly got more in return, including a formal say in the way things were run, and first pickings at any good freebies we could hustle. I think Committee Membership was a remnant of David's old idea of having a few people raise £2000 each, and it was not hugely popular, numbers reaching about seven or eight. The Club had always relied to a large extent on members dipping into their pockets, and the membership scheme was a way of formalising the level of contributions that were made. The most common concern expressed about the scheme was that there was no visible distinction between David's own money and the Club's. His answer was that anyone sufficiently interested to run it themselves in a different way, was welcome to try. This was a reasonably sincere response, indeed David often expressed disappointment that I did not want take over from him in running the Club, although he would never have given up control completely.

One result of the membership scheme was that posers who had no genuine interest in participating in anything that was actually dangerous, but who liked to be able to describe themselves as members of the Dangerous Sports Club, could buy the right to do so for £50. Just as you can subscribe to the National Trust and advertise your membership via car stickers etc, you could join the Club (arguably a less socially benign organisation) if you cared to contribute money to it. People who did join in this way were referred to as National Trust members, but this was not a completely disparaging term, and they often livened up social events. My only personal regret about the scheme is that many of them probably got rather poor value for money.

The scheme attracted about fifty members, which produced some income but hardly a fortune. We held weekly meetings at Biggles Wine Bar in St James'. Biggles is, sadly, now out of business, perhaps because it was so well hidden, in an obscure back yard, that you would have had trouble finding it with an *A-Z* map, sextant, compass, astrolabe and guide dog, even before getting drunk. A partner in this bar was a Club member; he was also a recreational pilot, hence the name of the bar. Living in Oxford, I could not attend many of these evenings. The bus fare alone was a fiver, and drinking in West End wine bars is beyond the pocket of a research student. But, when I did open my wallet and go, I had a good time.

We had a member called Alan Price, a helicopter pilot, who owned a fleet of penny-farthings and C5's which we would race around backstreets after closing time. But on the whole, socially, the way the Club was going appealed less and less to me. Most of the people who were in it when I had first become involved, had moved apart, and in the late-Eighties the Club was becoming increasingly London-centred.

The standard of the active jobs was also declining. David, often accompanied by me, made many approaches to advertising agencies and film production companies, which were awash with money if not imagination. We discussed many projects, but very little was ever put into practice.

Advertisers never quite got the hang of using innovative, dangerous sports, perhaps finding it harder to project their illusions and false ideals into the Real World, where a sham is quickly seen for what it is. In the more predictable modern spectator sports, in which money is a greater measure of success than gold medals, it is easier to purvey commercial delusions.

David was often very optimistic and excited when he felt he was about to be offered good money to do something really interesting and new. However, the contracts we actually landed were usually small, unexciting and poorly paid. In 1987 we were asked to take part in a publicity stunt at the opening of a new health and fitness club in central London. My part in this was to climb a mountaineering rope to the seventh floor gym and clamber in through a window. It made us a few quid, but I had to wonder why we bothered. I thought of this sort of thing as the commercial prostitution of the Club, and it would only be worth doing if the money was a lot better.

I was beginning to feel embarrassed about the Club. It had been so good, and had caught so many peoples' imagination, and yet it had fallen to this level. I was developing a certain amount of boredom and disillusion with the whole thing. I was still BASE jumping, but that was more a personal hobby than a Club activity. As for excitement within the Club, the ski races had long since finished, and after making some three or four hundred bungee jumps at several dozen shows over the last four years or so, I found it was getting to be a drag. At the time, Britain's biggest sporting icon was a man from Cheltenham with thick spectacles who had come last in the Olympic ski jump. I liked his enthusiasm, but 'Eddie The Eagle' wasn't my idea of a sporting hero. I began to lose interest in sport, and started concentrating on the less important things in life, like work and money. I had to be more single-minded about my research or I would never finish my thesis; and I badly needed to earn some hard cash.

However, we still embarked on occasional larger enterprises.

David had long nursed an ambition to create a giant inflatable, polythene, man-carrying sphere, or bubble, based on one he had seen a few years before at Borth, in Wales. It was the creation of a local pair of artists, and it could float on water or roll over land. A passenger sat in a little seat, suspended by lines from the outer skin. We reasoned that a larger version of this bubble would have a great deal of air resistance, and could reasonably be expected to roll happily over a cliff and fall quite slowly to the bottom.

The long-established Club tradition of promoting alcoholic drinks continued, when the distributors of a Japanese melon liqueur called Midori agreed to sponsor this project to advertise their UK product launch. Craig Marner of Gas and Equipment made the 60ft sphere. I sat down with old Club member Dave Turnbull, and we came up with a design for a two seater carriage with a small tea table, to be slung at the centre of the bubble in a device called a gimbal, like the mounting of a ship's compass. The gimbal consisted of concentric, swivelling rings of aluminium tube, able to rotate within each other in such a way that the seats would remain upright however the device rolled. It was suspended in the centre of the sphere by cables attached to strengthened points on the polythene skin. The gimbal was fabricated for about £1000 by Hugo Spowers. Years after their feud over the ski race, they were still suspicious of each other, so David and Hugo used me as an intermediary. I knew Hugo's bill was much less than the full professional rate for work in aluminium, but it was hard to convince David he wasn't being overcharged.

Managing the production and testing of this device was a lot of work for me, and I came to hate the gimbal. Assembling it was always a pain in the neck, and the aluminium tubes had to be treated very carefully to avoid damage. Similar devices, on a smaller scale, are now used as fairground rides, in which people swivel around in all directions. Ours was bigger than that, because of the need to accommodate a tea table, and the idea was for the passengers to stay upright while the gimbal rolled in all directions.

Craig Marner and his team carried out the first test inflation of the bubble at the factory in Oswestry. Once the bubble was inflated, the wind picked up slightly, and before it could be deflated again, it rolled away. The giant ball had so much wind resistance that tying down the tether lines had no effect. There is just no stopping a 60ft sphere of polythene in a breeze. Snapping the tether lines, it rolled right over a lamp post, which had only been erected that morning, flattening it completely. The workmen came back from their lunch break at a loss to know what had happened to it. The sphere eventually rolled up against an electricity pylon, was ripped on barbed wire, and finally deflated. Perhaps this was just as well – there was no obstacle between the pylon and the M54 over the next hedge – but the electricity board were not at all pleased about it.

The bubble was so badly damaged that a new one had to be made. The first outing of the 'Midori Melon Ball' Mark 2 was scheduled for 19th August, 1986. The idea was to launch it from close by Tower Bridge, so that it would drift through under the control of two tugs. Reporters and photographers from several newspapers gathered to watch it going through the Bridge.

We finished making the seats in the gimbal late the night before. We took the gimbal and the polythene bubble itself to the launch site very early in the morning. The deflated sphere was an extremely heavy and awkward bundle of polythene, and handling it required a team of half a dozen people. Inflating the 60ft diameter sphere took hours, because of the sheer volume of air to be moved. Assembling the gimbal inside the sphere was also time consuming, and we had to begin as soon as there was room inside the bubble for us to stand up. David and Hugo were to be the passengers.

We were running late because the inflation took so long, and began to worry that we would miss the few minutes that morning when Tower Bridge would be open. Meanwhile, Midori, the sponsor, had kindly provided free samples of their product, but since we'd decided it looked and tasted like brake fluid, nobody drank it – the only occasion I can recall that members of the Dangerous Sports Club ever turned down a free drink.

Eventually we finished the inflation and assembly and got the bubble launched. The tugs, which were supposed to maintain control over the bubble as it drifted through the bridge, were anxious to pull it through before the bridge closed. In their haste, they pulled rather too hard on the tether lines. The Melonball once again demonstrated the power of air resistance. The tugs were a nearly irresistible force trying to pull an almost immovable object, and something had to give. The tugs tore out the strengthened panels which the tether lines were attached to. Gaping holes appeared in the polythene and the bubble began to deflate in mid-river.

Because there were several large holes, deflation turned out to be much faster than inflation, and within about ten minutes, David and Hugo had to cut their way out of the plastic and try to get into a boat. As the bubble collapsed on top of them, they were caught between two skins of polythene, and there was a risk of drowning or suffocation. Struggling to cut their way out, they quickly became tired, sinking into the floating plastic sheet like men in quicksand. Hugo was pulled out by the tug, and then finally David, half drowned and close to panic, was rescued. The wreckage of the bubble and gimbal drifted to shore close by the bridge, and it took us the rest of the morning to get it out of the water. We had to cut it up in order to do so, and the skin was a write-off, although much of the gimbal could be re-used.

The press had taken a lot of pictures of the untimely end of the bubble's maiden voyage, and the sponsors were pleased with the coverage, which made almost all the national newspapers. We went back to Craig Marner, and got a third skin made. This time the plan was to cross (you've guessed it) the Channel. Sadly, the sponsors wanted the whole skin painted green. We had been able to see out of the first two bubbles, and quite a view it was – I had a ride across Edgbaston reservoir during a test of the second bubble – but the final bubble did not offer its passengers any view at all.

In July 1987 we set out to roll the Melonball across the Channel. The crew were to be Mark Chamberlain and David Kirke. We got to Dover the evening before, but it was already clear from the weather forecast that the wind would be quite wrong for a crossing. Even so, the Press were going to turn up, so we decided to go ahead with an inflation anyway. We duly inflated the bubble on the beach, and assembled the gimbal inside it. This was a dreary task given that we knew it was only an exhibition for some well-groomed bacteria from Wapping, and that there was no chance that the bubble would actually be launched. In fact, the press covered the story anyway, despite the lack of action.

The sponsor's PR company had arranged to provide refreshments for the Club members present and the reporters who turned up. As the bubble deflated over the next three hours, we took full advantage of this arrangement. Later, we found that the tide had come in and there was water under half of the deflating bubble. We got inside it, and found that the huge sheet of loose plastic laying over the sea water provided a strange new surface to play on. You would sink deep into the plastic-covered water until practically swimming, although quite dry. The PR company staff got in too, and we had a good laugh together waiting for the bubble to go down completely. Next day, they were rather more formal and less happy about the non-event which the crossing attempt had turned out to be.

In fact, the Melonball never did cross the Channel, or anything else. We made no further appearances for Midori, and the promotion was ended. The drink was a commercial flop anyway.

*

The Melonball project ended with a whimper rather than a bang, and it seemed this was happening to the Club itself. It was inevitable that those who had contributed most in previous years would drift away, as they moved on to other things. By the late-Eighties, several of them had moved abroad. David had pinned his hopes on new people replacing them, but I felt that the Club had lost its way. It had ceased to be a private club, and yet failed as a business. On the creative side, projects like the Melonball, which was based on an original idea over ten years old, didn't appeal to me any more. On the personal side, working with David was not getting any easier.

This was particularly true when, as in this case, we had to build the device three times and even then we still couldn't get it right. It seemed another big lost opportunity. As Marx said, history repeats itself, first as tragedy, then as farce – which shows how much we are creatures of habit, not learning.

18.

Oscar's Diner

'The reasonable man adapts himself to the world.
The unreasonable man persists in trying to adapt
the world to himself. Therefore all progress
depends on the unreasonable man.'
– George Bernard Shaw

There was to be one last hurrah. Despite the rows about
money between David and Aki during our trip to Tokyo,
the relationship with Aki did not end with that show.
Another TV show featuring the Club was arranged, this time to be
filmed at locations around the world. The planned programme
was to feature an opening scene in which Club members
descended from a helium-filled flying saucer-shaped balloon. The
following scenes involved bungee jumping and BASE jumping,
and a tea party which would be held on a platform placed on top
of a large hot-air balloon, which we would reach by helicopter.
The show was to end with the Club rolling the Melonball bubble
down a cliff into the sea. On paper it looked like a dream come
true, a chance to play with lots of toys and do some interesting
things, and get paid for it. But there were problems. I was not the
only one drifting out of the Club, and it was becoming difficult to
get reliable people to implement such projects. Nor would the
show's budget allow for buying large amounts of new equipment
and experimenting with new techniques.

David and Aki, together with Mark Chamberlain and Aki's
producer Shuji Homma, set off to look for locations in New York,
Los Angeles and Hawaii. Sadly, all that was achieved was a new
personal best for David in room service bills, and more acrimonious discussions with Aki. The location research was unsystem-

atic and unproductive. The financial backers realised that the whole plan was going off course, and they very nearly cancelled the project at this point. After a lot of discussion, it went ahead, but on a reduced scale and using fewer expensive locations. The flying saucer scenes were cut. They would film bungee jumps at a bridge in Japan, the bubble in Scotland, and a BASE jump from a cliff in Ireland.

Even on a reduced scale, the plans did not go smoothly. David hired some help to take the bubble to the Lecht, in the Cairngorm mountains, inflate it, and roll it down a mountainside. However, the wind was blowing uphill at the inflation site, and as before, the bubble could not be tethered against the wind. Half-inflated, it tore itself free of the trucks and cars it was tied down to and dashed itself to pieces against barbed wire. The third Melonball skin was completely destroyed and ended up as cloches in local vegetable gardens. There was no usable film of this disaster.

Aki's plan for the show made the cliff jump the climax of the programme. Mark and I had enthused about the cliffs of Moher in County Clare ever since we had visited Ireland to do some outdoor shows in 1985. The cliffs are sheer, and about 700ft high, although since there is no dry landing site at the bottom, a recovery boat is necessary. The plan was to hoist a catapult into position on top of the cliff, by helicopter. The rented catapult was the type used to launch unmanned target aircraft for gunnery practice. It had a short launching rail, and was powered by bungee rope.

David asked me to do the jump, even offering money, but although tempted, I refused. By that time I was no longer on very good terms with him, and did not want to get involved in any more projects he organised. The sheer impossibility of working with David had finally become too much for me. For the first half of the Eighties, the creative and exciting aspects of the Club had been to the fore, and we all hoped for great things. Later, it seemed that the good things became fewer and less exciting, and the hassles, sleaze, bad vibes and angry, late-night phone calls came to outweigh the fun. Also, I had completed my research project and needed time to earn a living and finish off my thesis, and did not want to spend any more time making Japanese TV shows. I became interested in more serious projects, such as the newly-announced plan to put a British astronaut in space, sponsored entirely by the private sector. Along with thousands of others, I applied for the job, and was among the 150 selected for preliminary medical and psychological screening. Here, I thought, was a chance to get involved in a properly organised adventure at last. Space flight! That should get the rocket fuel flowing.

For the cliff jump in Ireland, I recommended my friend Iain Kelly to act as David's parachuting adviser – someone to select the right equipment, pack it, and show him how to use it. David chose to use my parachute, which he had used before and was familiar with; I sold it to him.

On the appointed day, 25th January 1989, a helicopter carried the catapult to the cliff top, and a rescue boat stood by to fish David out of the sea. One important element was missing, though. The seat on which David would sit, and which would fling him forward along the rail, needed to be shaped to conform with his back and parachute pack, or the force of the catapult could injure his spine. The normal way to make such a seat is to use quick-setting polyurethane foam, which can be poured into a plastic bag, finds its natural shape, and then sets hard. However, the polyurethane had been left behind.

A more cautious person would probably have decided not to use the catapult without a proper seat, and simply made a running exit off the cliff in the normal way. Being David, though, he went ahead using the catapult. His launch over the cliff was filmed from several angles, including an aerial view from the helicopter. He sat, hunched, on the catapult; Iain Kelly gave him a few last words of advice, Shuji Homma signalled that the cameramen were ready, and the catapult was fired. Slow-motion video of the launch clearly shows the distortion his spine underwent; it was stressed beyond endurance, and suffered serious injury. He flew off the cliff, releasing his hand-held pilot chute immediately, and the parachute streamed out behind him. It opened perfectly, even though he was still moving horizontally faster than he was falling downwards, because of the high speed at which he had been flung from the catapult. He landed in the sea and was quickly fished out by the rescue boat.

David was to suffer the effects of the injury for a long time. The pain did not begin immediately, however, and true to form, he celebrated that night, and even managed to leave without paying either his hotel bill or the rental fee for the catapult. Later, though, when his doctor discovered the seriousness of the damage David had inflicted on his back, he had to undergo surgery. He was operated on successfully, but was left with continuous pain.

Some of the pain relief drugs he was prescribed had a depressing effect, so he often used alcohol instead, always his drug of preference. The combination of depression, heavy drinking and chronic pain brought him to rock bottom, without a home and without any means to earn a living. He went to France to avoid his creditors, who included British Airways, various shops, a builder, and a man whose American Express card he had seriously abused. Hertz were also after him, since he had rented a Mercedes from them in Rome and driven it to Carlisle. David's pigeons were coming home to roost in a big way. While he was in France, BBC Radio 4 made a half-hour programme about him for a series called *Face the Facts*, in which alleged rogues are confronted by their accusers.

The BBC reporter had plenty of material for the programme, but was unable to contact David himself to get an interview. Only a few people in England had David's phone number, and we were sworn to secrecy. In the end, I persuaded David to make a call – reverse charge, naturally – to Giovanni Ulleri, the reporter, and he was able to have his say in reply to the allegations. The programme was broadcast on St Valentine's Day 1991, and I thought it was actually quite positive. Although detailing a long trail of bad debts, it had a light-hearted tone, and whenever David's activities were described, the *Indiana Jones* theme music was played in the background. The overall impact of the programme was much less harsh than it might have been, but David was very depressed about it.

In his own words: Giovanni Ulleri

As an outsider looking in, it looked like a lot of jolly japes, with people in top hat and tails doing crazy things, drinking champagne and bungee jumping and so on, which is all very well for student kind of pranks, but when I started looking into it in more depth, I realised that in those jolly japes, some people did lose out. One particular case I felt quite strongly about was the stunt in Ireland. There was an Irish guy who did a lot of work on the safety of the stunt, arranging boats and so on, who was meant to be paid, and he's not a rich individual who can afford to be ripped off, he's just a little Irish guy. Part of the thing is the philosophy of the Club, whereby Kirke would say the big boys can afford it, American Express, the banks and so on, but these little guys can't afford it, and there were lots of little guys all the way through who got ripped off. That was the thing I found

156

offensive about it, but then some of the things that were done were actually quite incredibly brave, and I have a lot of admiration for them.

Not paying your bills isn't an art form. The arrogance wasn't the problem – that was just ordinary upper-class arrogance, but you simply can't go through life trashing little people. You others [in the Club] are responsible too – you let it happen.

David returned to Britain in April and was arrested. He was charged with several counts of fraud and given £10,000 bail. David's brothers and Chris Baker put up the money, and David was allowed out. He began to prepare his defence, which was that he had committed the offences while under the effects of personality-altering medication. He collected an impressive number of references from all kinds of people, stating that his offences were out of character, and supporting his case for clemency. Some of the references were so glowing they were actually over the top and couldn't be presented to the court. Despite this support, he could not deny that he had taken money from his accusers, and in fact asked for several dozen other offences to be taken into consideration. His case was that he had done it while his judgement was diminished – a sad thing to admit for a man who had lived for years on the edge of irrationality between adventure and lunacy, with only his judgement to hold on to. When his judgement failed him at the cliffs of Moher, in the Real World, the laws of dynamics and physiology had meted out their own, pitiless justice to him; now, at Horseferry Road magistrates court, the laws of man, hopefully tempered with mercy, would have their say.

The defence of diminished financial responsibility did not impress the bench. In December 1991, David was found guilty of fraud and sentenced to nine months imprisonment. As he had already spent some time in jail before his release on bail, he had only about half this time left to serve. However, in the time-honoured tradition of kicking a man when he is down, *Private Eye* printed a harsh piece about him in their next issue. They did not shrink from publishing the worst of the stories they had heard; there was no 'lovable rogue' impression this time.

Given that he had to be locked away, he was delighted to be sent to Reading jail, where Oscar Wilde had once been incarcerated. He wrote to all his acquaintances on notepaper headed 'Oscar's Diner'. When Mark Chamberlain and I visited him, he was a little embarrassed to be seen in such circumstances, but in some ways he seemed to gain personally from the experience of doing time. He was locked up with a wide range of other convicts, most of them better men than David in the eyes of the law, for they had smaller ideas and so had stolen less.

His personal decline mirrored that of the Club as a whole. Without him, and with the other leading members having drifted apart, it was no longer organised and co-ordinated as it was in the early and middle-Eighties. Those years were the heyday of the Club, in terms of participation, public recognition and fun. Despite tremendous missed opportunities – such as the Hollywood movie – a lot of things happened which entertained a lot of people, but the Nineties have seen no further expeditions or inventions, and the people involved are mostly scattered in pursuit of their own paths in life.

We may have been silly, irresponsible, in debt, and out of step with everyone else – but somehow that spirit struck a chord and resonated, and sometimes it still does. The Dangerous Sports Club did what the British have done several times before; invented a game that the rest of the world plays. Along the way, we provided a lot of innocent entertainment as well. All of us are older now and marginally less childish, but a leopard doesn't change his spots completely, and many are still active sports enthusiasts.

*

Meanwhile, I had not fared too well in my ambition to become an astronaut – or perhaps I should say cosmonaut, as it was a collaborative project with the Soviet Union. After making the final shortlist of about thirty individuals, I underwent a wide variety of tests, some more comfortable than others, and gave samples of many things that Nature did not mean to be sampled. I ran uphill for hours on a treadmill while breathing through a tube. I was X-rayed; my heart, eyes and teeth were examined (they didn't seem worried about my injured right eye), and I was probed in every orifice. There were dexterity tests in which I picked up tiny ball bearings using tweezers. There were several mental tests and endless psychological questionnaires with questions such as, 'Is your mother a good woman? Do other people like you? Would you rather be a bishop or a brigadier? What is your favourite colour?' I made a speech to an imaginary press conference and was interviewed several times. I wrote an essay, signed a contract, and promised my total commitment. It was all no use. I failed to get the job. Somewhere along the line, they decided that I wasn't made of the Right Stuff, or at least, that my stuff wasn't as righteous as someone else's. It was a disappointment, naturally, but not a crushing blow – I still had a life, and as one of the psychologists had told me, I was quite happy with it (I had decided not to tell them about my urge to leap off cliffs and bridges).

The project itself, called Juno in imitation of the American habit of naming space projects after mythological gods, was supposed to be paid for by commercial sponsorship, advertising and the sale of TV rights, in the Thatcherite spirit of the times. However, just as Thatcherism itself was finally hitting the rocks at that time, the reliance on private sector money for Juno was proving a fatal flaw in the scheme. The mission director, Peter Graham, failed to raise the money, and was then exposed as a fraud, who had obtained his job by telling an extraordinary pack of lies. He approached companies and asked them for vast sums of money to sponsor an exotic adventure – and when they turned him down, the whole project began to crumble. Although I was out of it by the time it hit rock bottom, it was all beginning to sound horribly familiar.

Peter Graham was sacked, and the Moscow Narodny Bank, the original financial guarantors, together with Glavcosmos, the Soviet space agency, looked for the door. With only a small fraction of the planned £16m actually raised, the project hung in the balance, and the two selected candidates found themselves half way through the cosmonaut training programme, fearing to be told at any time that the space flight was off. In the end, escaping cancellation by a whisker, the project went ahead on a shoestring, but with minimal press coverage or public interest. The first Briton in space – a food scientist called Helen Sharman – ended up working on routine Soviet space tasks, rather than the hoped-for (but not paid-for) British scientific experiments. This was sadly ironic, since the whole project had been started by a group of scientists who wanted to send their experiments into orbit. Helen spent a happy week in orbit, landing safe and sound. She should perhaps consider herself lucky to get back down to Earth at all – one of the Russians who went up in the same rocket got stuck in space for over a year. The unfortunate Sergei Krikalev was abandoned in orbit, sucking his protein paste while his entire nation collapsed and disintegrated beneath him, and the worn-out space station creaked its way round an indifferent world. By the time he eventually landed, he was too weak to stand up, the Soviet Union was history, his salary was worthless, and Moscow's great museum of space achievement had become an American car showroom.

Adventures? I can pick 'em.

19.

Into the Twilight Zone

'Happy are those who dream dreams, and are
willing to pay the price to see them come true.'
– Carl Boenish

There were faces dotted around the church I hadn't seen for years, many faces, all framed by black ties and sombre expressions. I was standing at the back, in a group of two dozen who had not found a place on the crowded pews. The little church had not been so well attended for a long time.

Following the family mourners, we moved out into the grave-yard and stood quietly while the coffin was lowered into the ground. Tommy Leigh-Pemberton had died in a late-night road accident in Zimbabwe. A man who saw the crash said, simply, 'Very fast – no brakes!' A tragic accident, of the sort that happens occasionally to those with a thirst for new experiences, who refuse to be restrained by caution, who take pleasures and face risks, who seize life with both hands, knuckles white. They know that if they are unlucky, the circus will be over sooner rather than later, but they could never take a ringside seat when there were lions to be tamed or a trapeze to swing on.

That he had been one of the most popular members of the Club was clear from the turnout of old members; it was, effectively, our first re-union since the 1980s. After the burial, naturally, we gathered together with his family to share his memory and catch up on personal news. A treasured family album was shown, filled with pictures of Tommy and his friends building a playground in a Romanian orphanage, bicycling to Australia, and on many other adventures, including a few that we in the Club had shared with him. We leafed through as memories came back of times we had spent together, good, bad, and outrageous. Tommy really had managed to avoid conformity with consumer culture, resisting its endless, mind-numbing onslaught, following his own spirit and truly being himself – a rarity and an example.

Around the room were many of my old Club friends that I had kept in touch with. Steve Smithwick, who had married Nina Knox-Peebles' sister and now has two children; Mark Chamberlain, about to go to the Moscow Film School for four years; Chris Baker, who is designing a radical new high-speed motorcycle; Hugo Spowers, who has built a business restoring vintage racing cars, and wants to start a Formula One team; David Kirke, working on his autobiography. We swapped news of others who could not be present, such as Alan Weston, who is building rockets in California, and Xan Rufus-Isaacs, who is a lawyer in Los Angeles. Then there were some old friends I had not seen for three or four years; Mike Fitzroy, now also married; Henry Robinson, who, like me, had gone into scientific research and a technical career; Alan Price, still flying helicopters and riding penny-farthings. It was a chance to exchange addresses, and inevitably the question was asked; what are you doing now? I had an answer; I was going to jump El Capitan – at last.

*

So, finally, I found myself on the overhanging rock at the top of El Capitan, half a mile above Yosemite Valley. In many places, BASE jumping is now becoming quite acceptable, but not in Yosemite. The Park Rangers still relish their role as the Spanish Inquisition of cliff jumping. A $2,000 fine, equipment confiscation, several days jail, and deportation faced me if I didn't make a fast get-away.

I had hiked up the mountain with a BASE jumping friend, and we slept under the stars at the launch point, a tiny ledge over-looking the great drop to the valley floor. The climb was a long and hard one, but really, that had been the easy part. Getting to this rocky ledge had actually taken me over fifteen years. With dawn coming, we put on our parachutes, gave each other a last check, and approached the precipice. The mighty granite mono-lith slopes downwards so steeply at the edge that we could not risk leaning over for a look. Only the jump would give us a clear view of what lay below – a case of 'leap before you look'. We hoped that, at 5am, the chances of the Rangers being on patrol at the landing site were small – although they have often staked out the area, and even used dogs to hunt down jumpers. I had come to Yosemite once before, hoping to make the jump, and been foiled by a stakeout – a failure which had weighed heavily on me ever since. The price we paid for jumping into the pre-sunrise twilight was a less clear view of the whole jump, and a higher risk of accidentally flying into a tree as we came in to land; for this price, we hoped to buy time to run, unseen, into the woods, and hide our equipment.

Sleeping out before the jump had been a calming and peaceful experience, which allowed time for reflection on the many things which had happened since I first dreamed of jumping here – a period which took in my whole adult life. As dawn approached, although the rocket fuel had begun to flow, I remained calm and cheerful, the best mood for BASE jumping. My partner took three short paces and disappeared over the ledge; I took a breath and started after him. The second step down the slope was the point of no return – I couldn't stop now, and as usual, I dumped some emotional baggage at this moment. This had been my dream since I first saw Carl Boenish's film back in 1980, and now, at last, it was happening. The burden of waiting was lifted from me; the failure last time was now erased, and it felt good.

With the last short step, over the edge, the step which constituted a Federal offence, the awesome beauty of the valley was spread before me. Like a surprise Christmas present, it was all the better for not having peeped until this moment. I seemed to hang in mid-air, frozen in the last starlight as the sun brought colour to the view, suspended as the twilight zone below became my Real World, framed by the immensity of the cliff and the depth of the space below me. That last short step, also the giant leap of my dreams, was a moment to treasure deep in the soul. The whole of civilisation is left behind when your foot loses contact with solid ground. Social structures, money values, authority, and all the lifeless rituals of hypocrisy we call politeness, are dimly remembered, if at all. So many years and so many miles long, my journey was truly accomplished only in that last step.

As if to show contempt for the laws of man which prohibit cliff diving, the law of gravity took relentless hold, and I began the steady downward acceleration. It felt like the smoothest motorcycle ever ridden; effortlessly, precisely, I gained speed and felt the wind ever stronger on my face. Easing forward into the tracking position, head down, arms by my side, I began to glide out from the cliff, as though flying across a vast, barren landscape of bare rock, faster and faster, yet in near-silence and half darkness. With every nerve alive, I was running flat out; mind, body and spirit as one, with no separation of thought from instinct, no distinction of flesh from soul. For twelve seconds, I flew out, away from the rockface, following my partner down towards the opening point, that invisible yet vital place at which cliff jumpers must throw their pilot chutes or very quickly run out of choices. With total focus on the moment, and the rocket fuel pumping round fast and hot, for those twelve seconds the mountain and the air were the whole universe. God! Perhaps if I'd never had the nerve to open the throttle fully, to pull out all the stops, I could have settled for a quieter life. It would have made getting life insurance a lot easier. With some reluctance, I threw out the pilot chute and, a second later, felt the tug of line-stretch.

Canopy open, I looked around and turned to fly along the cliff for a few hundred yards; this would help to conceal me from anyone below, who might have heard the opening. At the last minute, I turned out into the valley and flew down to the landing point. The valley floor is 4,000ft above sea level, and I expected the landing to be hard, but it turned out to be gentle enough, and I found myself standing once again on firm ground, burning with elation and breathing very quickly. I hid my parachute under a dead log and went away a discreet distance through the trees. I would come back for it later when I was sure nobody was looking. The sun was rising now, enough to chase away the last star, and I glanced up to the launch point 3,000ft above.

It had been worth the effort – saving for the tickets, the disappointment of the failed attempt, the risk of arrest, the steep, hot climb – for those twelve longed-for seconds of magical flight. Was anyone ever more free than this? Could anybody be happier? It had been so bitterly frustrating when the first attempt went awry, but I knew from my days in the Club that such an outcome was possible on any expedition. How many Dangerous Sports Club adventures had needed a second or third attempt? One lesson at least had sunk in; persistence is everything. Without it, whatever else you may have going for you, is thrown away. If I had given up the dream of jumping El Capitan because of early failure, I could not have blamed bad luck, but only my own lack of determination.

Peace came over me as I breathed the scent of pine and looked up once again. A fragment of a song lyric came into my mind:

> 'Poor is the man whose pleasures depend on the
> permission of another.'
> – Madonna (*Justify my Love*)

Also available in paperback from The Do-Not Press

Dancing With Mermaids
by Miles Gibson

'Absolutely first rate. Absolutely wonderful' – Ray Bradbury
Strange things are afoot in the Dorset fishing town of Rams Horn.
Set close to the poisonous swamps at the mouth of the River Sheep, the town has been isolated from its neighbours for centuries.
But mysterious events are unfolding… A seer who has waited for years for her drowned husband to reappear is haunted by demons, an African sailor arrives from the sea and takes refuge with a widow and her idiot daughter. Young boys plot sexual crimes and the doctor, unhinged by his desire for a woman he cannot have, turns to a medicine older than his own.

'An imaginative tour de force and a considerable stylistic achievement. When it comes to pulling one into a world of his own making, Gibson has few equals among his contemporaries.'
– *Time Out*
'A wild, poetic exhalation that sparkles and hoots and flies.'
– *The New Yorker*
'An extraordinary talent dances with perfect control across hypnotic page.' – *Financial Times*
ISBN 1 899344 25 X – £7

The Sandman
by Miles Gibson

"*I am the Sandman. I am the butcher in soft rubber gloves. I am the acrobat called death.*
I am the fear in the dark. I am the gift of sleep…"
Growing up in a small hotel in a shabby seaside town, Mackerel Burton has no idea that he is to grow up to become a slick and ruthless serial killer. A lonely boy, he amuses himself by perfecting his conjuring tricks, but slowly the magic turns to a darker kind, and soon he finds himself stalking the streets of London in search of random and innocent victims. He has become The Sandman.

'A truly remarkable insight into the workings of a deranged mind: a vivid, extraordinarily powerful novel which will grip you to the end and which you'll long remember' – *Mystery & Thriller Guild*
'A horribly deft piece of work!" – *Cosmopolitan*
'Written by a virtuoso – it luxuriates in death with a Jacobean fervour'
– *The Sydney Morning Herald*
'Confounds received notions of good taste – unspeakable acts are reported with an unwavering reasonableness essential to the comic impact and attesting to the deftness of Gibson's control.'
– *Times Literary Supplement*

ISBN 1 899344 24 1 – £7

BLOODLINES the cutting-edge crime and mystery imprint...

That Angel Look by Mike Ripley

'The outrageous, rip-roarious Mr Ripley is an abiding delight...'
– Colin Dexter

A chance encounter (in a pub, of course) lands street-wise, cab-driving Angel the ideal job as an all-purpose assistant to a trio of young and very sexy fashion designers.

But things are nowhere near as straightforward as they should be and it soon becomes apparent that no-one is telling the truth – least of all Angel! Double-cross turns to triple-cross and Angel finds himself set-up by friend and enemy alike. This time, Angel could really meet his match...

'I never read Ripley on trains, planes or buses. He makes me laugh and it annoys the other passengers.' – Minette Walters.
1 899344 23 3 – £8

I Love The Sound of Breaking Glass by Paul Charles

First outing for Irish-born Detective Inspector Christy Kennedy whose beat is Camden Town, north London. Peter O'Browne, managing director of Camden Town Records, is missing. Is his disappearance connected with a mysterious fire that ravages his north London home? And just who was using his credit card in darkest Dorset?

Although up to his neck in other cases, Detective Inspector Christy Kennedy and his team investigate, plumbing the hidden depths of London's music industry, turning up murder, chart-rigging scams, blackmail and worse. *I Love The Sound of Breaking Glass* is a detective story with a difference. Part whodunnit, part howdunnit and part love story, it features a unique method of murder, a plot with more twists and turns than the road from Kingsmarkham to St Mary Mead.

Paul Charles is one of Europe's best known music promoters and agents. In this, his stunning début, he reveals himself as master of the crime novel. ISBN 1 899344 16 0 – £7

BLOODLINES the cutting-edge crime and mystery imprint...

Fresh Blood II edited by Mike Ripley & Maxim Jakubowski

Follow-up to the highly-acclaimed original volume (see below), featuring short stories from John Baker, Christopher Brookmyre, Ken Bruen, Carol Anne Davis, Christine Green, Lauren Henderson, Charles Higson, Maxim Jakubowski, Phil Lovesey, Mike Ripley, Iain Sinclair, John Tilsley, John Williams, and RD Wingfield (Inspector Frost).

Fresh Blood edited by Mike Ripley & Maxim Jakubowski

Featuring the cream of the British New Wave of crime writers including John Harvey, Mark Timlin, Chaz Brenchley, Russell James, Stella Duffy, Ian Rankin, Nicholas Blincoe, Joe Canzius, Denise Danks, John B Spencer, Graeme Gordon, and a previously unpublished extract from the late Derek Raymond. Includes an introduction from each author explaining their views on crime fiction in the '90s and a comprehensive foreword on the genre from Angel-creator, Mike Ripley. ISBN 1 899344 03 9 – £6.99

Smalltime by Jerry Raine

Smalltime is a taut, psychological crime thriller, set among the seedy world of petty criminals and no-hopers. In this remarkable début, Jerry Raine shows just how easily curiosity can turn into fear amid the horrors, despair and despondency of life lived a little too near the edge.

'Jerry Raine's *Smalltime* carries the authentic whiff of sleazy Nineties Britain. He vividly captures the world of stunted ambitions and their evil consequences.' – Simon Brett

'The first British contemporary crime novel featuring an underclass which no one wants. Absolutely authentic and quite possibly important.' – Philip Oakes, *Literary Review*. ISBN 1 899344 13 6 – £5.99

BLOODLINES the cutting-edge crime and mystery imprint…

The Hackman Blues by Ken Bruen

'If Martin Amis was writing crime novels, this is what he would hope to write.' – *Books in Ireland*

'…I haven't taken my medication for the past week. If I couldn't go a few days without the lithium, I was in deep shit. I'd gotten the job ten days earlier and it entailed a whack of pub-crawling. Booze and medication is the worst of songs. Sing that!

A job of pure simplicity. Find a white girl in Brixton. Piece of cake. What I should have done is doubled my medication and lit a candle to St Jude – maybe a lot of candles.'

Add to the mixture a lethal ex-con, an Irish builder obsessed with Gene Hackman, the biggest funeral Brixton has ever seen, and what you get is the Blues like they've never been sung before.

Ken Bruen's powerful second novel is a gritty and grainy mix of crime noir and Urban Blues that greets you like a mugger stays with you like a razor-scar.

GQ described his début novel as:

'The most startling and original crime novel of the decade.'

The Hackman Blues is Ken Bruen's best novel yet.

Shrouded by Carol Anne Davis

Douglas likes women — quiet women; the kind he deals with at the mortuary where he works. Douglas meets Marjorie, unemployed, gaining weight and losing confidence. She talks and laughs a lot to cover up her shyness, but what Douglas really needs is a lover who'll stay still — deadly still. Driven by lust and fear, Douglas finds a way to make girls remain excitingly silent and inert. But then he is forced to blank out the details of their unplanned deaths.

Perhaps only Marjorie can fulfil his growing sexual hunger. If he could just get her into a state of limbo. Douglas studies his textbooks to find a way…

Shrouded is a powerful and accomplished début, tautly-plotted, dangerously erotic and vibrating with tension and suspense.

ISBN 1 899344 17 9— £7

BLOODLINES the cutting-edge crime and mystery imprint...

Perhaps She'll Die! by John B Spencer

Giles could never say 'no' to a woman... any woman. But when he tangled with Celeste, he made a mistake... A bad mistake.

Celeste was married to Harry, and Harry walked a dark side of the street that Giles – with his comfortable lifestyle and fashionable media job – could only imagine in his worst nightmares. And when Harry got involved in nightmares, people had a habit of getting hurt.

Set against the boom and gloom of Eighties Britain, *Perhaps She'll Die!* is classic *noir* with a centre as hard as toughened diamond.

ISBN 1 899344 14 4 – £5.99

Quake City by John B Spencer

The third novel to feature Charley Case, the hard-boiled investigator of a future that follows the 'Big One of Ninety-Seven' – the quake that literally rips California apart and makes LA an Island.

'Classic Chandleresque private eye tale, jazzed up by being set in the future... but some things never change – PI Charley Case still has trouble with women and a trusty bottle of bourbon is always at hand. An entertaining addition to the private eye canon.' – *Mail on Sunday*

ISBN 1 899344 02 0 – £5.99

Outstanding Paperback Fiction from The Do-Not Press:

Elvis – The Novel by Robert Graham, Keith Baty

'Quite simply, the greatest music book ever written'
– Mick Mercer, *Melody Maker*

The everyday tale of an imaginary superstar eccentric. The Presley neither his fans nor anyone else knew. First-born of triplets, he came from the backwoods of Tennessee. Driven by a burning ambition to sing opera, Fate sidetracked him into creating Rock 'n' roll.

His classic movie, *Driving A Sportscar Down To A Beach In Hawaii* didn't win the Oscar he yearned for, but The Beatles revived his flagging spirits, and he stunned the world with a guest appearance in Batman.

Further shockingly momentous events have led him to the peaceful, contented lifestyle he enjoys today.

'Books like this are few and far between.' – Charles Shaar Murray, *NME*
ISBN 1 899344 19 5 – £7

The Users by Brian Case

The welcome return of Brian Case's brilliantly original '60s cult classic.
'A remarkable debut' –Anthony Burgess

'Why Case's spiky first novel from 1968 should have languished for nearly thirty years without a reprint must be one of the enigmas of modern publishing. Mercilessly funny and swaggeringly self-conscious, it could almost be a template for an early Martin Amis.' – *Sunday Times.*
ISBN 1 899344 05 5– £5.99

Charlie's Choice: The First Charlie Muffin Omnibus by Brian Freemantle – *Charlie Muffin; Clap Hands, Here Comes Charlie; The Inscrutable Charlie Muffin*

Charlie Muffin is not everybody's idea of the ideal espionage agent. Dishevelled, cantankerous and disrespectful, he refuses to play by the Establishment's rules. Charlie's axiom is to screw anyone from anywhere to avoid it happening to him. But it's not long before he finds himself offered up as an unwilling sacrifice by a disgraced Department, desperate to win points in a ruthless Cold War. Now for the first time, the first three Charlie Muffin books are collected together in one volume.

'Charlie is a marvellous creation' – *Daily Mail*

The Do-Not Press
Fiercely Independent Publishing

Keep in touch with what's happening at the cutting edge of independent British publishing.

Join The Do-Not Press Information Service and receive advance information of all our new titles, as well as news of events and launches in your area, and the occasional free gift and special offer. Simply send your name and address to:

The Do-Not Press (Dept. SADSC)

PO Box 4215

London

SE23 2QD
or email us: thedonotpress@zoo.co.uk

There is no obligation to purchase and no salesman will call.

Visit our regularly-updated Internet site:

http://www.thedonotpress.co.uk

Mail Order

All our titles are available from good bookshops, or (in case of difficulty) direct from The Do-Not Press at the address above. There is no charge for post and packing. (NB: A postman may call.)